Tools of the Trade

Competing on God's Team

TOOLS OF THE TRADE

Ben Johnson, Tools of the Trade

ISBN 1-929478-78-X

Cross Training Publishing
P.O. Box 1874
Kearney, NE 68848
(308) 293-3891

This book is manufactured in the United States of America.

CONTENTS

REWARDS

FOREWORD

As athletes we face temptations of kinds. Whether it is pride, anger, bitterness, or jealousy towards teammates, we are constantly bombarded with difficult situations. Our goal should be to meet these challenges prepared with the knowledge of what God expects from us. In Ben Johnson's Tools of the Trade, he guides us through the temptations of this world using Godly advice, great present-day illustrations, and examples from Jesus' life.

I hope that as you read through these devotionals you will find the wisdom that lies in God's Word and the peace that comes from faith in Jesus Christ.

Remember, whether in sports or life, fundamentals are essential. Tools of the Trade will sharpen your Christian fundamentals and help you become a more valuable player on God's team!

Chris Burke
Houston Astros

INTRODUCTION

There are many elements that go into developing a great athlete and winning team. An often overlooked, but vitally important element is the spiritual development-especially in our win at all cost society. Athlete or not, we all take time for ourselves at varying degrees physically, emotionally, and socially. Yet the spiritual component is the one that brings them all together. My hope for you by going through these daily devotionals and studying the Playbook (Bible) these three questions will be solidified in your life:

1) Whose team are you on in life?
2) What position does the Head Coach have you currently playing?
3) Will your performance at the current position merit an award some day?

These devotionals are a collection of chapel material I have used over the last seven years working with high school, college, and professional athletes here in Austin. They are great to use over the course of a season with a team, or on your own as you further study to compete as our Lord and Savior competed, while here on this great playing field. The scriptures for each devotional are the basis. Read, study, and commit them to memory, for that is what will change your life! This book would not have been possible without some key people: First my wife for her friendship and constant support, dad and mom who placed a Biblical foundation within me growing up even though I so often rebelled, Marcia Chamblee, Cindy Hume, and Susan Hartsfield for their help in editing, Connally HS and Concordia University for allowing me to borrow the pieces I needed for the cover, and the many friends who allowed me to use them and their experiences as illustrations. Most importantly, Jesus Christ, my personal Savior and Head Coach for changing my life!

Ben Johnson

GOD'S TEAM

Growing up, competition was part of my daily life. The process was this: the two best players were captains, they would pick their teams and the game was on. In life, the process is not much different. The top two players, in this case God and Satan, are leading the teams. What once was Satan serving God changed as Satan sought after the desire to be "in charge" to call all the plays, to lead his own team. No longer did he desire to serve God. There are only two choices. To serve on a team whose coach's game plan is complete destruction of your life, who lies all the time, and whose outlook is not very bright. Or to play for a coach who knows you are going to make errors yet still loves you, has a plan for your life to mature you and make you better, and promises a wonderful ending. It would seem the choice is pretty easy. Yet many choose each day one team over another. Which team will you play for in your lifetime?

In Whom Do You Trust?

"Some trust in chariots and some in horses, but we trust in the
name of the Lord our God."
PSALM 20:7

I once heard a story told by a preacher about a man in North
Dakota. It was January and this particular man was attempting to
walk across a frozen pond for the first time. He doubted he would
make it across, but after examining all the evidence: cold, ice, and
distance to travel, he gives it a go. The pastor told the story about
another man in the same place attempting to do the same thing.
This man was confident he would make it across. The only
difference was he was attempting to cross in March with thinning
ice and warming temperatures. Who do you think made it across?
The confident man in March, or the doubting man in January?

In whom or what do you trust? King David trusted in God over
the size of his army or the weapons he possessed. He knew where
real victory came from. Do you trust in your abilities to provide for
your future? If so, you are not playing by God's rules. In the story
above, it was not the size of faith that made the difference. The real
difference was what the men put their faith in. Put your faith in
something stable and firm. If you do, each step will be a faith
developing process as you cross through life.

Daily challenge: What are some other things you are guilty of
putting your trust in?

Varsity or JV

"Here there is no Greek or Jew, circumcised or
uncircumcised, barbarian, Scythian, slave or free,
but Christ is all, and is in all."
COLOSSIANS 3:11

The varsity and junior varsity teams for most start in high school.
The two teams represent the same school and are even coached by
the same coaches. Having the two teams allow more kids to compete in athletics than would normally get the chance. Coaches are
able to build up their younger players giving them valuable game
experience in preparation for the future.

As Tommy Nelson, pastor of Denton Bible Church in north
Texas, put it, "...there is no junior varsity and varsity on God's
team." We are all on God's team. There may be players on the team
with greater levels of maturity and knowledge, but these only come
from living a long consistent life of struggle and study of God's
playbook. Some churches today operate with a junior varsity and
varsity system. If you do not give a certain amount of money, raise
your hands during worship, or pray as they pray, then you must be
on junior varsity. You may not be as "spiritual" as they are. In fact,
you probably have sin in your life and need to confess it. Paul
emphasizes IN CHRIST we are all equal. IN CHRIST we are all
equal and the Head Coach has a key position unique to the abilities
He has given us.

Daily Challenge: In what ways do you allow God to use your abilities?

IDENTITY

"But he answered his father, 'Look! All these years I've been
slaving for you and never disobeyed your orders.
Yet you never gave me even a young goat
so I could celebrate with my friends.'"
LUKE 15:29

A good coach knows the value of all his or her players. Even though
they may say all are equal, it must be demonstrated. It is not defined
by the amount of playing time, but rather in the enforcement of
team rules, policies and communication. Likewise, the players must
have the right perspective about themselves. Do they feel they are
insignificant to the success of the team because of a particular position they play? Great teams are made of players making contributions
not just on game day. You may not be a starter, but with the right perspective, you can make an impact in your team's performance.

In Luke 15:29, the older brother displayed the wrong perspective. He viewed himself as a servant rather than a son. He got his
self-worth by what he did rather than who he was as a son. Do you
know as a Christian that God views us all as sons and daughters? He
is the type of coach that loves regardless of how small our bank
account might be or what our title is at work. In fact, He sent his
only true son to die for you and me when He knew we would deny
Him (Romans 5:8). Where does your identity come from? Is it your
job, sport, appearance, money, or God's Word? Whatever it is, it will
set the tone for your outlook on life.

Daily Challenge: Do you view yourself as a son/daughter of God?
How should this change your attitude?

GOD CHOSE US!

> "You did not choose me, but I chose you and appointed you to go and bear fruit-fruit that will last. Then the Father will give you whatever you ask in my name."
> JOHN 15:16

Every spring, the National Football League puts on the college draft. Teams spend millions of dollars scouting, analyzing, debating, and measuring these college football players. The goal is to find the right guys to fill their needs. It is every football players' dream to be selected in the first round. However, with it come instant wealth and prestige as well as major responsibility and pressure. Once the player is chosen, he is the "property" of that team and they begin to seek a return on the investment they have made. Often, a player once selected will hold out from signing a contract for more money and miss out on valuable time preparing for the season.

Did you know you are God's #1 draft pick? This is what John 15:16 says. God chose you (and me)! We are His! We didn't find Him, He found us. He also desires a return on his investment in the form of our bearing fruit. Don't turn down the chance to be on God's team. Moreover, don't be a holdout. He has a spot He desires to put you in. It may not be in your desired position or have the title you want but our responsibility is to be faithful wherever he places us. After all, He has the best retirement plan ever known!

Daily Challenge: How does knowing God chose you affect your self-esteem? How about your attitude?

STAND FOR GOD

"For if you remain silent at this time, relief and deliverance for the
Jews will arise from another place, but you and your fathers family
will perish. And who knows but that you have come to
royal position for such a time as this?"
ESTHER 4:14

One of the most used clichés in sports is, "We are taking it one
game at a time." What athletes and coaches are saying is 'today is a
new day.' Yesterday is gone, win or lose, today is a new opportunity.
All athletes can do is focus on today bringing all they can so they
might be better tomorrow. Be it one game or one day, this is a great
approach to take. Particularly in sports, when the monotony of
practice, and the pressure of games get overwhelming.

In a sense, this is what Mordecai was challenging Esther to do
in verse 14 of Esther chapter 4. Facing an awful destruction of the
Jewish people at the hand of King Xerxes, someone within the
nation of Israel had to step up. Either Esther was going to stand by
faith for the Lord's people in the face of the king risking death or
shrink back quietly. What would you do? Today is the day to stand
for God. Not tomorrow or some time in the future when your circumstances are more favorable. Don't rest in your past triumphs,
but remember them and press on to a greater reliance on God
today.

Daily Challenge: Are you on God's team? Would other people say
you are? Why?

HOME FIELD ADVANTAGE

"But if serving the Lord seems undesirable to you, then choose for
yourselves this day whom you will serve, whether the gods your
forefathers served beyond the River, or the gods of the Amorites,
in whose land you are living. But as for me and my household, we
will serve the Lord."
JOSHUA 24:15

When the term "home field advantage" is brought up as it relates to
sports, what comes to your mind? To me it is how the Texas Rangers
baseball team is able to hit with a greater average at home than on
the road, or how the University of Nebraska football team has a 270
consecutive games and counting sellout streak.

In the Bible, Joshua knew the importance of winning at home.
The nation of Israel had taken their eyes and trust off God. Their
priorities were out of order and someone needed to step in and call
them out. Joshua was that someone, he would not follow the
majority. He proclaimed that not just himself, but his entire house
was going to serve the Lord (verse 15). Isn't it amazing when a man
stands for God his entire household is affected? Have you taken a
similar stand? Being on God's Team may require some sacrifices.
You probably won't be in the majority and even your family sometimes may not fully understand. But what an advantage you will
have if your home is committed to following God...a far greater
advantage than any sports team could ever have.

Daily Challenge: Cultivate time today to strengthen those relationships at home. Solidify your relationships to your family and God.

HEARING THE COACH

"Why is my language not clear to you?
Because you are unable to hear what I say."
JOHN 8:43

In baseball, the manager will call the plays from the dugout or 3rd base-coaching box. Basketball and football coaches call the plays from the sidelines. Even though the other teams are in plain sight, they do not know what is being called because they are not on the same team. In all three cases, the player must know what each sign means so they can do what the coach wants. If they do not, he or she will cause the team to be unsuccessful. The signs go out before every play, but are useless if the player does not know and do them.

In the same manner, our spiritual head coach sends signals out every day. How do you know what he is communicating? The formula is quite simple as John 8:47 states: "He who belongs to God hears what God says. The reason you do not hear is that you do not belong to God." Having a relationship with anyone involves communication. I may know Peyton Manning, but I do not have a relationship with him because I do not communicate with him. Do you hear what God is saying to you? There are many ways he speaks to us. More than likely, we will not hear Him audibly, but through prayer, reading his Word, circumstances, and other Christians He speaks. We are only able to reach our full potential on God's team by hearing what he would have us to do. It is very simple. Take time to listen for His direction today.

Daily Challenge: Can you think of some times when God has spoken to you?

WHICH DIRECTION?

"There is a way that seems right to a man, but in
the end it leads to death."
PROVERBS 14:12

It was the 1929 Rose Bowl. The "Granddaddy of them All" they call
it. Georgia Tech beat California in what was a defensive struggle by
the final score of 8-7. The real story took place in the 2nd quarter.
Georgia Tech had the ball deep in their own territory when they
fumbled. Scooping up the football for the Cal defense was Roy Rea-
gles-that is Roy "Wrong Way" Reagles. Getting confused in the play,
Roy scampered 70 towards the Tech end zone before his own teammate tackled him at the 1-yard line! The ensuing series turned into
a blocked punt and safety for Georgia Tech making the difference
in the final score.

In the game of life, we have two end zones we can head towards.
Matthew chapter 7 describes them as the wide and narrow gates. I
am talking about one end zone of a personal relationship with Jesus
Christ. The other is the one of opposition towards Team Jesus.
There is no middle ground. As Proverbs 14:12 says the way that
"feels" right may not always be the right end zone. Our world is
consumed with "doing what feels good" regardless of the results.
Examine in which direction you are headed in life. Roy Reagles was
convinced he was going in the right direction, only to be badly mis-
taken. It is, however, a good thing he was playing in a football game.
The game of life has eternal consequences.

Daily Challenge: Which end zone are you headed towards? Are you
bringing others along with you?

PRACTICE

In the sports world, discipline is a key quality to possess. The word discipline has a negative connotation. It is not the glamorous part of playing sports. Truth is, more hours are spent practicing than performing. Generally, it is the athlete with good practice habits who perform at a higher level. In this section, we will focus on some spiritual practice habits. Just as coaches design a daily plan for their team's practice, our spiritual head coach has a practice plan for us. It does not guarantee ease, wealth, and health. It will, however, set us on the right course for performing in the game of life. In today's times, we need more Christians who will choose to live a disciplined life.

BIBLE STUDY

"Do your best to present yourself to God as one approved, a work-
man who does not need to be ashamed
and who correctly handles the word of truth."
II TIMOTHY 2:15

Coaches who focus on the fundamentals have teams that perform consistently. They know when their players get into a habit of doing the right things that confidence will develop. When an athlete is playing with confidence, often times he or she will perform at a level they never knew they could reach.

Paul left young Timothy with many nuggets of wisdom. Knowing his time on earth was coming to a close, he wanted to be sure Timothy had all the instruction needed to perform consistently as a Christian leader. The practice fundamental here was for Timothy to "correctly handle the word of truth." God's Word is often mishandled today, and usually it is from a lack of study and proper teaching. No matter what position or role God has placed you in, your focus should be on His Word. By knowing His Word, His nature is revealed helping you to become more effective in your assignments.

Daily challenge: Do you take serious how import it is to handle God's Word correctly?

PRAYER

"Pray continually."
I THESSALONIANS 5:17

Prayer and sports quite often are linked together. A team will gather before a game for prayer, asking God for safety from injury and His blessing on their play. Some gather during the game when a key play is about to take place. Many times opposing players will kneel together at the end of a game in football after a hard fought game.

Someone once said, "Praying is harder work than doing." Meaning, it is harder for us to stop, get quiet and still to seek help and direction from God than to keep putting our nose to the grindstone asking God to bless "our" work. In Thessalonians, Paul is instructing the people to pray all the time. All the time, meaning not just before important events or before a meal. Paul knew the importance of constant communication with God. We do not have to be in a church building to talk to Him. We can reach Him day or night. Prayer is a key habit we need to practice if we are hoping to max out as Christians.

Daily Challenge: How often do you talk to God? Of what does the conversation consist? Is it one-way or do you take the time to listen?

WITNESSING

"But in your hearts set apart Christ as Lord. Always be prepared to give an answer to everyone who asks you to give the reason for the hope that you have. But do this with gentleness and respect."

I PETER 3:15

A well-known athlete once said, "You don't have to be great to get started, you just have to get started to be great." In order to be a multi-Olympic Champion swimmer, Josh Davis spent hour-upon-hour training. All the hours of training would in just seconds determine who was the fastest in the world. Josh got to see the fruits of his labor by winning 3 gold medals in the 1996 Atlanta Olympics. By training his body, pushing through soreness, and listening to his coaches, Josh Davis became a champion.

Just as Josh had to train his body to become a champion swimmer, we too must train ourselves to be witnesses of the gospel. This is what Peter the Apostle is emphasizing to all Christians. We all are accountable to tell what Christ has done in our lives at any time and at any place. It does not matter how skilled a communicator we are, how much knowledge we have, or do not have, or how insignificant we think we may be. We are simply to be ready to speak with gentleness and respect. Every once in a while, just as Josh did, we will see the fruits of our training when we lead someone to a personal relationship with Christ.

Daily Challenge: When was the last time you told someone what Christ has done in your life?

OFF-SEASON TRAINING

"Preach the Word; be prepared in season and out of
season; correct, rebuke and encourage-with
great patience and careful instruction."
II TIMOTHY 4:2

Teams that excel have players who commit to off-season training. In most cases coaches cannot force the players to work out. It's the committed ones that view the off-season as a chance to improve their game and reach their full potential.

The same goes for God's team. There is no off-season. We do not "check out" for a week or two and do what we want to do. Paul was teaching young Timothy this very principle-to be ready at all times. We never know who is watching our actions. We could be called upon to talk about what God has done and is doing in our own life. Just when we think we can relax and coast it the time when we will have an important witnessing opportunity. Will you be ready?

Daily Challenge: If you had the opportunity to share your faith with someone who is not a Christian, would you do it? What would you say?

AUDIENCE OF ONE

"Whatever you do, work at it with all your heart, as
working for the Lord, not for men."
COLOSSIANS 3:23

Julie was one of those players coaches loved. She was the first one
to practice, and the last to leave. She loved winning a lot of basketball awards, but she was never satisfied with her play. She was the
best athlete on the court, but this year she determined was going to
be different. She had purpose. It started at FCA camp the summer
before when she began a personal relationship with Jesus Christ.
She now had a reason for playing basketball beyond the headlines,
trophies, and fans.

When competing in the game of life, we have one motivation
on God's team. Whether in the working world, a student, or retired
we have one goal. Making other goals is important, but they should
never approach the status and priority of #1. It's about doing everything all out for God. Colossians 3:23 read and applied correctly,
leaves no room for a Christian to be lazy. "…Work at it with all your
heart…" Why? Because our work is for God, our head coach, the
creator, and not for any human.

Daily Challenge: For whom do you work/play/study/live?

WORK ETHIC

"Therefore, I urge you, brothers, in view of God's mercy, to offer
your bodies as living sacrifices, holy and pleasing to
God-this is your spiritual act of worship."
ROMANS 12:1

Roger Clemens and Nolan Ryan are two of the greatest pitchers of all time. What has allowed them to have success for a long period of time? Work ethic. Yes, they are talented, but one could argue it is their disciplined workout regimen that has made them hall of fame material. Training their bodies, pushing them to the limit, so they could excel.

The writer of Romans had the same thing in mind when he came to chapter 12. He pleads with the Christians in Rome, and challenges us today to worship God with our body. We don't have to be in a church building to worship God. He designed us to worship him every day, in all we do. This includes our speech, thoughts, what we listen to, our attitude, and actions. Simple things, which we control, and have the potential to bring glory to God with.

Daily Challenge: In what ways can you worship God today?

ROLE MODEL

"Whatever you have learned or received or heard from me,
or seen in me-put it into practice. And the
God of peace will be with you."
PHILIPPIANS 4:9

One characteristic of a great team is their practice habits. When the stars of the team are the hardest workers pushing the others in practice, game performance will be high. A well-known NBA player (a former MVP and role model for many teens) once proclaimed how unimportant practice was to his performance. Since those statements, his team has not come close to the level of play they once had.

In contrast, one of the key players in the early church states to us just how important our spiritual practice is. Paul urged the Philippian church, which he started, to "put into practice" the example he lived before them. Not that he was the standard to live by, but he was a role model of how the Christian life is to be lived.

Daily Challenge: What are your "spiritual" practice habits? Who are some role models in your life? Are you becoming a role model?

2 KINDS OF PRACTICE

"Therefore, since we are surrounded by such a great cloud of witnesses, let us throw off everything that hinders and the sin that so easily entangles, and let us run with perseverance the race marked out for us."
HEBREWS 12:1

Being a college athlete requires hours of practice…so much so that the NCAA puts limits on practice times by allowing only a set number of hours per week for individual and team practice. The individual work allows a coach to focus more attention on each player. This is where a coach can teach on key details helping to sharpen the individual's performance. Team time allows for the entire unit to improve their performance. A team that practices well together will play well together. These two kinds of practice are also key in our spiritual lives.

The writer of Hebrews illustrates the importance other teammates can have in our lives. By surrounding ourselves with like-minded people who want to glorify God, we can experience great growth. Being able to discuss our struggles, sharpen each other with God's truth, and lift one another up in prayer will help us in our quest to finish strong. No team can max out without struggling together, and learning what each other does best.

We must also spend time alone with God. Psalm 4 shows how vital it was for King David to spend time in quiet, being still. As a coach works on specific fundamentals with a player individually, God will build directly into our lives when we are alone with Him.

Daily Challenge: Are you spending enough quality practice time in both areas: team and individual?

INTRODUCTION

MENTAL GAME

In order for an athlete to compete at the highest level, he or she must have the proper mindset. They are prepared for success when they have answers to questions like: What are your goals? Do you get your identity out of your performance? Many Christian athletes have the mindset that if they pray, go to church, don't go out and party, then they will play well and God will bless them. They are trying to draw a correlation between their performance and God's love for them. Aren't we grateful God is not like that? I know I am. God's love does not depend on our performance on or off a field. His love is unchanging. He is not concerned with stats, awards, or recognition.

In this section we will study the importance the mental game has in the athletic world and in the game of life. Are you an athlete who happens to be a Christian or a Christian who happens to be an athlete? Do your actions reflect it?

BE GENUINE

"Consider the blameless, observe the upright;
there is a future for the man of peace."
PSALMS 37:37

They are more common now than ever. Rules committees have tried to stifle them a little, but they still occur every Sunday in the fall. What are they? They are post touchdown celebrations and they come in all styles. Probably the most common style is an athlete kneeling in prayer and pointing to the sky. What first comes to my mind when I witness this scene is to wonder if that person really knows God. Would their lifestyle off camera represent a genuine attitude of praise to God? Anyone can praise God in the end zone.

King David struggled with this issue of being genuine. Though not a perfect man, he strived to live a genuine life before God. As he looked around Israel, he saw many who acted one way on the Sabbath but did whatever they wanted the rest of the week. We don't have this problem today though. Or do we? Examine yourself. How often do you open up your Bible during the week? What God has done for us in the form of his Son deserves a life of genuine, sincere, real faith on our part. King David believed so.

Daily Challenge: Are you genuine? What would others say?

MIND PLAN

"Set your minds on things above, not on earthly things."
COLOSSIANS 3:2

"Ninety percent of baseball is physical, the other half is mental."
-Yogi Berra

Isn't this quote from Berra true? Not just for baseball, but in every sport. An athlete's mental approach to the game will usually dictate the outcome, even more than the amount of talent they possess. If they think they are going to lose, lacking confidence going in, it will probably happen. The mind controls the rest of the body.

Likewise as Christians, what we allow into our mind will dictate our actions. The apostle Paul urged the Corinthian people not to have "even a hint of sexually immorality." He knew where it could lead. One thought can give way to action, action to sin, and sin to spiritual death. There is also a multitude of earthly consequences: divorce, diseases, pre-marital sex, broken homes and so on. All of these are against God's design and will for our lives. We are to have a game plan ready when the sinful temptations occur. We must not allow them to float around in our mind or we will act on them.

Daily Challenge: What is your game plan when sinful thoughts come?

MEASURING

"Let us fix our eyes on Jesus, the author and perfecter of our faith,
who for the joy set before him endured the cross, scorning its
shame, and sat down at the right hand of the throne of God."
HEBREWS 12:2

Being named to his third All-Star team in 2004, Lance Berkman
had arrived as one of MLB elite players. In the world's eyes, he
achieved success because of his statistics, not to mention making
millions of dollars. Lance, however, chose to measure success in a
different way. In a July 2004, Sports Spectrum article Lance was
quoted as saying, "First and foremost, I'll know I'm successful if I
instill the values of Christianity and a relationship with God into
my children. The recognition of Christ and his values is the most
important thing for my family and me. If I can do that and have an
impact on people around me - my teammates, my extended family, and anybody I come in contact with - and show them the love of
God, then I will have been a successful person."

Regardless of what profession you are in, if you are a Christian,
then there is only one way to measure success. It is exactly as Lance
described: a relationship with Christ combined with sharing Him
with others in love. It is not in the size of your bank account, the
number of awards you have received, or any milestone you can
accomplish. "Fix your eyes," on Jesus and allow your relationship
with Him to be the measuring element of success.

Daily Challenge: What are some ways you have determined success
in your life?

ROUTINE

"Be joyful always; pray continually; give thanks in all
circumstances, for this is God's will for you in Christ Jesus."
I THESSALONIANS 5:16-18

The game of golf is one that requires great patience. To be great
takes talent, time, and instruction, but any golfer will tell you it is
the mental part of the game that will eat you alive. Most golf teach-
ers will teach you to simplify approach the game by getting in a
routine and staying with it. Fundamental things such as the proper
grip, a balanced stance with correct alignment, and tempo are the
building blocks for that elusive consistency in golf. While it may not
guarantee a frustration free round, following the routine, will produce more consistent play.

Similarly, the apostle Paul gave the people of Thessalonica in
chapter five a routine to follow while striving to do God's will. If we
follow this routine consistently, it allows them to live right in the
middle of God's plan for their life. This routine still works today in
our lives. It requires great mental focus. We are to rejoice in our sit-
uation we are placed in life. We are to come to God in prayer, not
just before a meal, but all throughout the day. We are to give thanks
always, for as Christians, we know we have unlimited things for
which to be thankful. As we follow the routine, not as a robot, his
plan will be fulfilled in our lives.

Challenge: What are some of your normal daily routines? How can
the routines Paul mentions fit within your day?

ATTITUDE

"Your attitude should be the same as that of Christ Jesus:"
PHILIPPIANS 2:5

As Christians, just what should your attitude be when you are in the middle of fierce competition? If the opposing team's pitcher hits your star player while he or she is at bat, or someone on your team spreads a nasty rumor about you that is not true, how do you respond? Do you follow your teammates rushing the mound looking for payback? You don't want to let them down or risk being considered a coward right? Or, in the other instance, do you counter back with rumors about your teammate that are in turn untrue to make them look bad?

The Bible does not give a specific step to take in these particular instances. It does, however, give us a model to follow that is wise. Our example is Jesus, and Paul's description of his attitude. It is today's Bible reference in which Jesus' attitude can be described as a humble, obedient servant. He was God's son, 100% man and 100% God. He had it all, yet gave it all up for us. He did not seek revenge on those who put him on the cross. He saw past those who were against him and loved them, despite the sin they were committing. This is our model, our goal, and our example to look to when we are faced with an attitude decision.

Daily Challenge: Will you choose today to model your attitude after Jesus? Is there someone you are close to that exhibits that type of attitude?

GO THE DISTANCE

"We demolish arguments and every pretension that
sets itself up against the knowledge of God, and we take captive
every thought to make it obedient to Christ."
II CORINTHIANS 10:5

Len Bias, Maurice Clarett, Roy Tarply, and Lawrence Phillips...the list goes on. For what are these guys know? None of them ever reached their full athletic potential and finished well as it pertains to their athletic careers. They all had a world of talent. They were all on top of, or heading to the top of their sport at one time, yet got sidetracked. What was it that kept them from "going the distance" in their careers and reaching their potential? Most would say it was consistently making bad decisions in life and relationships.

Spiritually speaking, why do many not reach their full potential and finish well? We hear story after story of pastors who are so gifted yet comprise in the area of character and are disqualified. We discover that it doesn't matter what position you are in or what your title is, anyone can fall. As Paul points out, the beginning of the end is in the mind. When we allow a thought of lust, greed, envy, etc. to rest in our mind there will be a negative result. This "negative result" takes on another name called "sin" that separates us from God. It is the presence of sin that keeps us from maxing-out in God's eyes. Commit today to keep inventory of every thought. Don't allow a wrong one to set up shop in your mind today.

Daily Challenge: What is your plan for every sinful thought that enters your mind?

CONFIDENCE

"So do not throw away your confidence; it will be richly rewarded."
HEBREWS 10:35

It was the 1980 Winter Olympic Games. The Russian hockey team was easily the favorite to take gold medal. One year earlier they had dominated the NHL all-star team 6-0 in a deciding series game. The USA team was made up of college players who, who though good, lacked the experience many of the international teams possessed. Just to medal would have been a great accomplishment for USA. As the games began, team USA played well, developing confidence in an early tie and some key wins. Beating the Soviets in a dramatic game, and eventually taking the gold medal, the USA hockey team achieved one of the greatest moments in American sports history. How key were those early round victories? Without them, Team USA may not have had the confidence to play they did later in the games.

The writer of Hebrews hammers home the importance of living with confidence. Someone once described it as the memory of past success. Being able to recall the moments in life when God was faithful, where we overcame a trial, or were able to make a difference, can carry us through overwhelming odds. God promises as we continue to persevere developing confidence, we will be "richly rewarded." Our confidence does not depend upon our abilities or circumstances, but only in the master plan of our Head Coach.

Daily Challenge: In what other things besides God are you guilty of putting confidence?

THE PLAYBOOK

In sports terminology the playbook is a team's manual that includes the plays, policies, rules, and goals. Once an athlete becomes part of a team, he or she is given "the book" to study and memorize. Failure to do so will probably result in decreased playing time, a missed signal, and in professional sports some sort of monetary fine. It is even worse for a player to lose his or her playbook. In spiritual terms, I am talking about the Bible. It is God's instruction book for the game of life. Few Christians take the time needed to know what the Bible says and apply it. This section is designed for you to understand more about the Bible and what its purpose is for your life. Do you know where your playbook is at all times?

MEDITATION

"Do not let this Book of the Law depart from your
mouth; meditate on it day and night, so that you may be
careful to do everything written in it."
JOSHUA 1:8

In the sports world, coaches are fired and hired daily it seems. In the 90's, the Dallas Cowboys had just won two Super Bowls, yet their head coach was fired because of an ego clash with the owner. Major college and professional coaches are faced with intense pressure to win above all else. What makes it even harder is when a coach is asked to replace a legend. Just ask Frank Solich who replaced Tom Osborne at Nebraska, or Jimmy Johnson who took over for Don Shula with the Dolphins. Neither coach lasted more than 6 years after taking over for legendary coaches.

Joshua knew a little bit about replacing a legend. Moses had led the nation of Israel out of Egypt, given them the 10 commandments from God, and continued across the Sinai Desert only to give over leadership to Joshua right before entering the Promised Land. Joshua had a tough task ahead of him replacing a great "coach." All throughout chapter one of the book of Joshua, God gives him encouragement and a clear directive on how to be a successful leader of this nation: meditation on the playbook. Reading, knowing, understanding, and living God's Law would guarantee Joshua success in the specific role he was placed. Are you struggling with confidence in the roles you are in? Follow God's plan for Joshua and see if the same will not hold true for you too!

Daily Challenge: What could happen if we spent time seeking to understand God's playbook and live it out today?

DIRECTION AND DISTANCE

"Your word is a lamp unto my feet and a light for my path."
PSALM 119:105

In the 2004 golf season, Phil Mikelson took his golf game to another level. Considered at the time the best golfer to never win one of the four major tournaments, Phil broke through in Augusta winning the Masters. What was one of the keys to Phil's win? He diligently studied the course, adjusting his game accordingly. Knowing the yardages, where he wanted to be positioned for each shot, combined with smarter play, set him up to be successful.

Likewise, God's playbook gives us clear direction in life as to where we should be positioned. Just as golfers cannot succeed without their yardage and rulebook, the Christian cannot succeed without his or her Bible. It is the lamp shining to tell our feet where to go. It is the light revealing where to aim our lives. It was all this for the writer of Psalm 119. All throughout his Psalm, he proclaims his dependence upon the "commands", "statutes", "laws", and "word" of God. While others around him persecuted him (v86, 95, 110, 161), the writer remained devoted to God, by putting hope in His Word.

Daily Challenge: Can you proclaim today what the writer in Psalm 119:147 proclaimed?

ABSOLUTES

"His divine power has given us everything we need for
life and godliness through our knowledge of him who
called us by his own glory and goodness."
II PETER 1:3

Three major components of a team's playbook are goals, instructions, and rules. These are all very clear and understandable for all the players to know what is expected of them. You might say there is no "gray" area when interpreting them. They are black and white. If a player fails to follow a rule, and instead does what they want to do, the whole team will suffer. The head coach, usually having lived in the shoes of his or her players, made up the playbook, and has a good idea of what should be in it. Players can take great comfort in the fact that all they have to do is follow the playbook, and the team's goals will be reached.

All throughout our spiritual playbook (Bible), there are clear absolutes for us to follow. Hundreds of them are in the form of promises from our Head Coach. Others reveal His true nature and how he relates to us. In Psalm 34, there are 16 promise filled statements. In Psalm 37, we can count over 25 Biblical promises. In Corinthians 10:13, God's promise through Paul is, no matter what we go through in life, it will not be more than we can handle and ultimately we are promised a way out. Consider what Jesus proclaims in John 15. Peter ties all the promises together in II Peter 1:3-4. We are to hold onto them, build our basis for living on them. Not because of what they say, but because of who they came from.

Daily Challenge: What other promises/absolutes do you hold on to from God?

GET ACTIVE

"Do not merely listen to the word, and so
deceive yourselves. Do what it says."
JAMES 1:22

AC Green was as consistent as they come in the NBA for over 15 years. Playing for many playoff teams, having three championships, and currently holding the record for consecutive games played, he was a true "Iron Man." All of these accomplishments are great, but the thing for which AC was most noted throughout his career and today is his stand for sexual abstinence. So often, famous athletes encourage people to make good decisions, stay away from drugs yet they do not do it themselves. AC not only encouraged abstinence, but also lived it out until the age of 38 when he married.

There is a fine line in our Christian walk between knowing what is right and actually doing it. In Romans chapter seven the apostle Paul was brutally honest when talking about this battle that occurs within us every day. "I do not understand what I do. For what I want to do I do not do, but what I do I hate" (Romans 7:15). This is the battle: to put our faith into action, resist temptation, and live apart from our old sinful nature. We must choose to gossip or not to gossip, to speak an encouraging word, or to be kind and loving to our families. These are just a few things we KNOW we should do; yet often times do not. God has given us his playbook not just to read, but to LIVE BY. As James urges us to do, let's put it into action today.

Daily Challenge: Will you put your awareness and knowledge of God's playbook into action today?

UNCHANGEABLE

"But the man who looks intently into the perfect law that gives
freedom, and continues to do this, not forgetting what he has
heard, but doing it-he will be blessed in what he does."
JAMES 1:25

Being a college or professional football player requires a great deal
of discipline. For example, the constant study required to know
your team's plan as well as your opponent each week is extremely
time consuming. As introduced in this section, this is done in the
form of the learning the playbook. Defense, offense, and special
teams all produce their own playbook and all change from week to
week. The players are expected to not just know it, but also repro-
duce it out on the field despite the constant changes each week.

In contrast, God's playbook never changes. Even though it was
completed almost 2,000 years ago, the game plan for us is the same
today. This is why James, the half-brother of Jesus, urges us to "stare
at is intently." Why? He gives us three great reasons: because it is
perfect, because we will be blessed, and because we will gain freedom. We will have freedom to know the game plan and have enjoy-
ment putting it to use. Just as coaches design playbooks for their
players, our Head Coach has designed an unchangeable, perfect
plan for us today.

Daily Challenge: Why do you think it is important to study God's
playbook?

TEACH IT

"...and how from infancy you have known the holy
Scriptures, which are able to make you wise for salvation
through faith in Christ Jesus."
II TIMOTHY 3:15

One of the greatest basketball players of all time did not become great overnight. Neither did he attain his skills all by himself. Sure, he spent hours practicing alone, but Pistol "Pete" Maravich had a dad who spent time with him teaching him the game. He spent hours as a young boy dribbling and shooting while other boys were out trading baseball cards or riding bikes. When he would master a skill, his dad would come up with something more challenging for Pete to work on to elevate his game.

Similarly, young Timothy did not learn Biblical truth overnight and all by himself. He benefited from a mother and grandmother who spent time pouring into him God's truth. The Jewish custom was to start teaching kids when they were five, but some Biblical scholars believe Timothy started learning before then. The teaching of God's playbook is vastly overlooked today. Instead, many pastors give message after message with entertaining video clips and catchy three points that all rhyme. Find someone who is committed to teaching you God's playbook. It is the only thing that will truly change your life.

Daily Challenge: Does the church you attend teach the Bible? Do you have a Timothy to whom you can teach the Bible?

INSPIRED AND EQUIPPED

"All Scripture is God-breathed and is useful for teaching, rebuking, correcting and training in righteousness, so that the man of God may be thoroughly equipped for every good work."
II TIMOTHY 3:16-17

John Wooden has influenced thousands, if not millions, of athletes, coaches, and everyday people thru his life. As head basketball coach at UCLA, his teams were legendary. Yes, the wins and championships were what got the majority of the attention, but more importantly were the lives he inspired and helped equip for life beyond basketball. Coach Wooden had talented players that he taught Biblical principles to in hopes of turning out mature, Christian men.

The same pattern Coach Wooden followed started many years ago. Throughout history, God's playbook has been inspiring and equipping an untold number of people. Here in II Timothy, Paul reveals to us a very key truth: all scripture comes directly from God and has a purpose. This means from the first chapter in Genesis to the last verse in Revelation. Many religions and denominations do not follow this vital spiritual and absolute truth. We cannot pick and choose which parts of the Bible we "feel like" believing. It's all of it or none of it. If applied correctly, the Playbook will inspire and equip us for the task our Head Coach has assigned.

Daily Challenge: Does the church you attend believe ALL of the Bible is true?

TEAMMATES

When chemistry exists among teammates, the team can reach a higher level of play than they may have ever dreamed. This was true for the 1979 Pittsburgh Pirates who adopted the song, "We are Family" because it described the way they felt about each other. They rode that moniker all season long, coming back from a 3-1 World Series deficit to the Baltimore Orioles to win it all!

In this section we will study the importance of depending upon our spiritual "teammates." You may not always get along with every one of them, but our Head Coach commands us to love one another. This is just one in the list of directions He gives us as we relate to our spiritual teammates.

SURROUND YOURSELF

"They risked their lives for me. Not only I but all the
churches of the Gentiles are grateful to them."
ROMANS 16:4

In the sport of boxing, one of the more entertaining times of a
match is the boxers' march to the ring. Making his way to the ring
through the crowd of people, the boxer is accompanied by his
"entourage." The idea of the "entourage" is for the boxer to sur-
round himself with people in whom he trusts and relies-people
who have been a help throughout his life as well as for the challenge
that are ahead.

Chapter sixteen is an often-overlooked chapter in the great
book of Romans. With so many great sections all throughout the
book, this ending chapter gets brushed over like a genealogy listing
in the Old Testament. Chapter sixteen is a listing of Paul's
"entourage," the people that had provided, encouraged, and minis-
tered to Paul in his life's service to Christ. Some were people Paul
had even led to Christ. He realizes these teammates' share in the
great work he has done. Here is another example of someone making a difference for God's team, not going at it alone. Paul was surrounded by and gave credit to the teammates with whom he was
working alongside. Make sure to have some solid teammates
around as you go through life. Without them, you will not be following the Head Coach's game plan.

Daily Challenge: Why is it we sometimes believe we can accomplish more by ourselves than by working with others?

TEAM CHEMISTRY

"How good and pleasant it is when brothers live
together in unity!"
PSALM 133:1

The 2004 Texas Rangers excelled beyond what the "experts"
thought. After multiple years of finishing the season at the bottom
of the division, they were in the race until the final week. There
were many reasons for their change in play-one being team chemistry. Gone from the year before were the superstar players with the
big contracts and egos. The team was made up young players and
some veterans who mixed well. No one player captured the entire
spotlight-rather it was a TEAM.

King David knew a little about team chemistry by the life within his own family. His own son Absalom, consumed with the need
for power, tried to overthrow him as king-causing the nation of
Israel and the family much grief. Here in Psalm 133, David writes
of the pleasant nature that occurs when teammates in Christ live in
harmony with one another. He probably is remembering the days
when he and Jonathan, King Saul's son, were close (I Samuel 20).
On God's team, no one person is more important than any other.
We are all created in His image and for His purpose. How sweet it
is when we lay our ego and selfishness aside to live for the glory of
our Head Coach together.

Daily Challenge: Are there some members on God's team with who
you are not at peace? What can you do today to change it?

GET ALONG

"Let us therefore make every effort to do what leads to
peace and to mutual edification."
ROMANS 14:19

What is the first thing that comes to your mind when someone
brings up former teammates Shaq and Kobe? Is it two of the greatest basketball players to ever play the game and won 3 championships together? For me, it is what might have been, had ego and
pride not driven them apart. They had a great run going, yet they
could not get along for the benefit of each other and the team. If
they had, who knows what they could have accomplished side by
side.

Having differences with people is not uncommon. Here in
Romans, Paul is addressing the very issue as he encouraged the
Christians to do whatever it took to get along with one another. If
it were enough to just live in peace, we could live in our little world
and not bother anyone. The problem is that is only half of what we
are commanded to do. We are called as teammates to also "mutual-
ly edify" one another. This means to encourage, pray for, and listen
to one another. Notice that this requires the big "E" word: EFFORT.
It is not going to always be easy. If it were, Shaq and Kobe would
probably still be reeling off championships. If we are able to get
along with our spiritual teammates, just imagine the victories we
may be able to win for our Head Coach.

Daily Challenge: When in arguments with other believers, what is
more important: the relationship or the argument?

FELLOWSHIP TOGETHER

"Again, I tell you that if two of you on earth agree about
anything you ask for, it will be done for you by my
Father in heaven. For where two or three come together
in my name, there am I with them."
MATTHEW 18:19-20

In the Texas Longhorn 2002-2004 college football seasons, there were many highs and very few lows. As usual on a team so large, with many contributors, and there was two who were key players on the "Special Forces" teams. Both started out as walk-on players, just happy to make the team, but in 2004, both earned full scholarships. Richmond McGee and Stevie Stigall would tell you they felt they were on the team for a reason. The reason was to be an example of Christ to their teammates. It was to keep each other accountable in their actions as well as praying for their teammates. It was to share their faith on trips when asked, to lead their FCA huddle on campus, and encourage other athletes to do the same.

What these two guys had throughout their days of playing, is what is called fellowship: spending real time dealing with real issues literally in the presence of God. Jesus Himself promised in the book of Matthew that whenever two or more got together in His name (fellowshipped), He would be there among them. Want to spend your time in the presence of God? There is no secret formula. Simply spending time in fellowship with other teammates in Christ for the right purpose will bring about His very presence.

Daily Challenge: Who are the ones with whom you spend time in fellowship? How consistent are you in doing it?

DISPLAY KINDNESS

"Get rid of all bitterness, rage and anger, brawling and slander, along with every from of malice. Be kind and compassionate to one another, forgiving each other, just as in Christ God forgave you."
EPHESIANS 4:31-32

Severe hazing of freshman athletes is becoming a thing of the past. While they may still have some extra responsibilities to do, it is nothing like it used to be. Feelings are hurt, alliances are formed, and team chemistry will not exist, causing the team to be made up of older players against the new ones.

Can you imagine if when a person joins God's Team by trusting Christ the very same people who are to be their teammates immediately ridicule them? That doesn't happen. What if because of their appearance or prestige, they are given a warm welcome of fellowship over someone who is not as affluent? Now wait a minute, this DOES happen and far too often. We on God's Team are all guilty on some level of forgiving people we want to like us and holding grudges against ones we don't. We are guilty of telling others how we were wronged by someone else. We are guilty of displaying kindness and hospitality to those who look like and act like we do, but not to people who may be a little different. Our reference today gives us a clear guideline of what our actions should be towards other teammates: being kind, compassionate, and forgiving to all. What is our basis for doing so? It's not if we feel like it or have the ability. It's because God forgave us through the efforts of His son, Jesus.

Daily Challenge: Is there a person today you need to forgive? For what are you waiting?

CONSIDER WHAT YOU SAY

"Do not let any unwholesome talk come out of your mouths, but
only what is helpful for building others up according to their
needs, that it may benefit those who listen."
EPHESIANS 4:29

Athletes, coaches, and fans in the sporting world often allow emo-
tion to control their behavior. This is displayed in the almost care-
free nature of the use of curse words. Individuals claiming to be
devout in their faith, "lose their mind," during competition. To go
a step further, major college and professional athletes are now conditioned on how to address the media before and after games. For
example, what to say, what not to say, and how to say it are all
points of emphasis when being taught to discuss team related issues
with others.

What we say or don't say affects the people we are around. Paul
gives us a good guideline to follow here, "say only what will build
them up according to their needs." To know another's needs
requires listening and knowing them. You do not have to be a psy-
chologist with years of training to be an encouragement to someone in need. Neither do you have to have your master's degree to
pull aside a friend in love and help set them straight. Neither Jesus
nor the disciples had any formal training. It requires being led by
God's Holy Spirit, taking our eyes off of ourselves, and being available. Consider what you say today, using the ability to speak to
build up another one of your teammates in Christ.

Daily Challenge: Can you think of someone who does a good job
of modeling this verse? If so, then learn from their example.

BE AN ENCOURAGER

> "When he came to Jerusalem, he tried to join the disciples, but they were all afraid of him, not believing that he really was a disciple. But Barnabas took him and brought him to the apostles. He told them how Saul on his journey had seen the Lord and that the Lord had spoken to him, and how in Damascus he had preached fearlessly in the name of Jesus."
> ACTS 9:26-27

The year was 1947 and major league baseball was about to undergo a major change. In that year, a young and very talented Jackie Robinson crossed the color barrier becoming the first African-American ball player in major league baseball history. Jackie had to endure more than most men have to in their lifetime, in the way of insults and threats for what he did. More than once, Jackie had a well-known teammate step up and come alongside him to show his support of Jackie to the fans and other ball players. Pee Wee Reese, captain of those Brooklyn Dodgers, laid his pride and favor with fans down to support Jackie.

Here in Acts 9, the apostle Paul was trying to cross into the ranks of the disciples in Jerusalem. Having formerly been in opposition to the disciples and anyone who followed after Christ, Paul was now a changed man. Few believed it except for one man who put his reputation on the line for Paul to testify. His name was Joseph. Joseph, because of his encouraging, selfless nature had earned the nickname "Barnabus" which literally means, "Son of Encouragement"(Acts 4:36).

Daily Challenge: Can you think of someone today who is in need of encouragement?

BE A GOOD TEAMMATE

"And let us consider how we may spur one
another on toward love and good deeds."
HEBREWS 10:24

He was a bullpen catcher in the minds of many fans but Dylan
Freytag was a key part of the 2001 Texas Longhorn baseball team.
Dylan was known for encouraging teammates, inviting guys to
team chapel, and taking time to listen. On the practice field, Dylan
was an example of hustle and hard work. He became intent on
putting his faith in Jesus into action and therefore was a difference
maker. Did Longhorn opponents look upon Dylan as someone to
look out for and scout? No, but ask any member of the Longhorn
team and each would tell you he brought great value. He could have
been bitter and stirred up dissention among players, but instead, he
consistently displayed the qualities of a good teammate.

In this verse, the writer of Hebrews is encouraging us all to take
on the attitude of a Dylan Freytag as we interact with our spiritual
teammates. It's not about living our lives to improve our status here
on earth in order to gain greater attention. Instead, we are to "consider" thinking about specific ways in which we can come alongside
to assist our teammates. For example, being available to listen, challenge, and encourage others, or being willing to serve in the shadows while someone else gets the attention. It could be something as
simple as giving above our regular tithes to another teammate with
a burden to go on foreign missions.

Daily Challenge: Have you been a good teammate lately or are you
stuck looking for your own headlines?

ACCOUNTABILITY

"As iron sharpens iron, so one man sharpens another."
PROVERBS 27:17

The 1996 New York Yankees were a team filled with classy veterans, as well as some up-and-coming stars. The MVP in the World Series that year for the Yankees was their closer John Wettland. Occupying the setup role to get to Wettland, was a young pitcher by the name of Mariano Rivera. Taking Rivera "under his wing", Wettland taught him what it meant to be a closer on the highest stage. Since then, Mariano Rivera has become the greatest closer of all time, with the most saves of any post-season pitcher.

The Yankee bullpen has not since reached the same level of dominance it had in '96. They benefited from 2 great talents sharpening each other as teammates to perform at a championship level. Here in Proverbs, King Solomon gives us a pattern for performing at a championship level in life: accountability. Solomon was able to understand that without having someone close to call us out when we are wrong, challenge us to live with Christ-like character, and encourage when we have been through a rough time, that we will never truly succeed. Just as iron must be hit up against another piece of iron to get a sharp edge, we too must spend time rubbing shoulders with other teammates in Christ who can sharpen us.

Daily Challenge: Who are the ones in your life who sharpen you?

INTRODUCTION

UNIFORM/EQUIPMENT

In every sport, the athletes competing must either have a uniform or right equipment. Some need both. Golfers must have long pants and a collared shirt. Soccer players wear soccer cleats and a team uniform. Can you imagine going to a basketball game and one of the players was wearing shoulder pads and a helmet?

In this section, we will study the uniform and equipment needed to compete and win on God's team. Many Christians leave the uniform hanging in their locker, only to put them on about two hours a week. They need to be put on every day. Why? As II Timothy 3:17 says: "so we can be equipped for good works." It is not possible to be a difference-maker on God's team without putting on the uniform. Not wearing the equipment properly will allow the opposition to be successful in any attack.

BEING PREPARED

"Therefore put on the full armor of God, so that when the day of
evil comes, you may be able to stand your ground, and after you
have done everything, to stand."
EPHESIANS 6:13

In baseball, a catcher knows at some point in the game he is going
to get hit by the baseball. It is inevitable. The first thing you teach a
young catcher is to face it head on. The second he turns his body or
head is he opens himself up to getting hit where there is no protection. Serious injury and/or missed playing time could be the result.

As we have studied and know, no one wants to be in the dugout
when it comes to competing in athletics, or in our spiritual life-
especially when it is preventable. Ephesians tells us, just as a catcher knows he or she is going to get hit with that baseball, we know as
Christians we are going to be attacked by the opposition. Both are
inevitable. The response should also be the same, being prepared to
face it head-on with the correct equipment. In the ensuing days, we
will study the pieces of our spiritual equipment needed for battle.
As you will see, they do no good if we do not face the battle head-
on. There is no protection on either the side or back of us. The
Head Coach designed it this way for He wants us to stand our
ground. This demonstrates our faith in His power and plan for our
life. Don't be surprised when hardship comes, the game plan
assures us it is headed our direction.

Daily Challenge: Can you think of a time when you were unpre-
pared for the opponents' attack and it led to compromise in your
life? How about when you were prepared?

BELT OF TRUTH

"Stand firm then, with the belt of truth buckled around your waist,"
EPHESIANS 6:14A

The only known sport to have a rule pertaining to a belt is boxing. It is not something that buckles around the waist of a boxer, but the line below which no punch can be thrown. By punching below the belt, a boxer can lose valuable points in a round that can ultimately decide a fight. Often times, boxers will wear their shorts higher than normal so as to guard against the "low blow." One of the first reminders the referee will give to the boxers before the fight is to keep it clean with no low punches.

The very first piece of equipment we are told to have on as Christians is the "belt of truth." The Bible doesn't spend a lot of time describing exactly what this belt is except that it is to be buckled and worn around our waist. This belt is described as one of truth. How can truth be a defense for us from day to day? First, by knowing the truth and next by standing up for what IS truth. Truth exists in the Playbook. There is, "The way, the truth, and the life," in John 14:6 where Jesus is referring to Himself. Also, we can have freeing peace as we tell the truth to one another. Are you a person of truth? How do you react when something other than truth is spoken? Notice the belt is the piece of equipment that holds everything else in place. However, it must be buckled and worn correctly in order to keep the opponent from landing a "low blow."

Daily Challenge: What are some ways in which you can stand for truth today?

Breastplate of Righteousness

"…with the breastplate of righteousness in place,"
Ephesians 6:14b

There is a great contrast in who today's elite athlete gives credit to for his or her accomplishments. They are all talented, putting time and effort into reaching the top, and being the best. For example, Lance Armstrong will tell you his own hard work, will, discipline, and doctors led to success. Curt Schilling, on the other hand, when asked after World Series with the '04 Red Sox, acknowledged it was God who granted him the ability, strength, and desire to reach the top of his game.

Who is right? It has to be one or the other for it cannot be both. In the arena of our daily spiritual battle, our teammate, the apostle Paul, commands us as a drill sergeant to put on the "breastplate of righteousness." One problem-on our own, we are not righteous. The Playbook clearly states in Romans 3 that none of us are righteous. Therefore, we must put on the righteousness of Christ. Because of what Jesus did for us on the cross, we are declared righteous in God's sight. Notice there is nothing of our own ability that can make us right with God. In Paul's day, a soldier in battle without a breastplate had vital organs wide-open for any opponent's attack. In our spiritual battle, without Christ's righteousness, we are wide-open to all accusations. We have no protection of our own. Put on the righteousness of Christ today and allow Him to cover over what the opponent may try to expose.

Daily Challenge: What does it mean to put on the "righteousness of Christ?" Can you see an advantage of doing this every day?

ARE YOUR FEET READY?

"…and with your feet fitted with the readiness that
comes from the gospel of peace."
EPHESIANS 6:15

Throughout the 1990s, there were two running backs in the NFL
who were head and shoulders above the others: Barry Sanders and
Emmitt Smith. Though they both were successful, they had different running styles. Emmitt was the between-the-tackles, resilient,
"wear-the-opponent-down" type. The opponent may have been
able to get their hands on him, but he would keep his feet churning
running through tackles for extra yards most backs could not get.
Barry was the escape artist, home run hitter. By contrast, Sanders
would juke, spin, jump, and reverse field to go for 50 yards!

In spiritual terms, our feet must be ready for action. If Emmitt
and Barry had ever quit moving those feet, then the defenders
would have gotten them down. Paul again instructs us to be ready;
reminding us that opposition is coming. The key here is not to be
ready to run, but to stand. Notice, as with the other pieces of the
armor, our feet must be fit correctly. There are many "things" in the
world trying to give us peace. Only one will allow us to stand when
hardship or opposition comes. This is the gospel of Jesus Christ.
From where does your peace in life come? If, as a Christian, it is
coming from the money you possess, the position you play on a
team, then you are not ready as Paul instructs us to be. Today, put
on the gospel of Jesus that will anchor you with peace.

Daily Challenge: What are some things in your life that can give
you a false sense of peace?

Shield of Faith

"In addition to all this, take up the shield of faith, with which you
can extinguish all the flaming arrows of the evil one."
EPHESIANS 6:16

Joe Montana had the faith of his coach and teammates. As a quarterback for the 49ers and Chiefs, his performances with the game on the line are legendary. Thus, Joe earned the nickname "Joe Cool." Amidst blitzing linebackers, loud fans, and little time, his performance only got better, usually propelling his team to a victory.

In the hours of our daily life when pressures build, how do you respond? Is it by working harder, cutting corners, and doing whatever you need to do to get by? Or do you step behind the shield of God's faithfulness? It is described as "great" faithfulness in Lamentations 3:23. So massive it extends up to the clouds in Psalms 36:5. The type of shield Paul is describing here is only effective when facing opposition directly. He is describing the Roman shield in combat. This was a full body-length shield. It was covered in leather and soaked in water so as to extinguish any flame-tipped arrows from the enemy. It was made even more effective when lined up with other shields to form a wall of defense, as lineman forming a pocket for the quarterback. Why was Joe Montana so effective under great pressure? Because he had done it all season long in practice and in games. Relying on God's faithfulness in the tough times requires that you have a history of doing so. Having others to stand alongside you will only help make the battle easier to overcome.

Daily Challenge: On a separate piece of paper or in a journal, write out some ways God has been faithful in your life.

HELMET OF SALVATION

"Take the helmet of salvation…"
EPHESIANS 6:17A

In week one of the 2002 NFL season, the Cleveland Browns were playing the Kansas City Chiefs. With the Browns leading late, the Chiefs were making one final drive for a chance to win the game with a field goal. Breaking through the line was Dwayne Rudd, a linebacker seemingly helping to stop the Chiefs as time expired. Before the play officially ended, Rudd tore off his helmet and threw it a few yards in celebration of the game being over. What Rudd failed to remember was an NFL rule of removing your own helmet is a 15-yard penalty and the game cannot end on a defensive penalty. Brown fans and players went through agony as the Chiefs were given those yards, putting them in field goal range and yes…one more play, as the Chiefs banged in the long field goal. Moral of the story: keep that chinstrap buckled until the final horn sounds.

This is also true in our spiritual life. We can have the other pieces of the armor on, but without the helmet, our minds are open for attack. The Playbook describes it as the "helmet of salvation." The salvation experience is the key to unlocking a personal relationship with Jesus. Jesus is our salvation! We should never forget it, but rather it should be a great memory we replay. Paul is reminding his teammates in Ephesus to keep that chinstrap buckled. He wanted them to use not just their feelings, but also their minds when living for Christ.

Daily Challenge: Are there things you allow to enter your mind that cloud your decisions?

ON THE OFFENSIVE

"…and the sword of the Spirit, which is the word of God. And pray in the Spirit on all occasions with all kinds of prayers and requests. With this in mind, be alert and always keep on praying for all the saints."
EPHESIANS 6:17B-18

The St. Louis Rams in 2000 were described as a team with "play-makers" at every position. That year, these "weapons," led the Rams to a thrilling Super Bowl win.

We have come to the last pieces of equipment, by the title; you know they are the offensive weapons. All the pieces Paul has described to this point have been defensive weapons. In verse seventeen and following, he describes the weapons of God's Word (the Playbook) and prayer. Is God's word meaningful to us today? The writer of Hebrews thinks so describing it as, "living and active, sharper than any double-edged sword." (Hebrews 4:12) In an earlier section, we studied the Playbook. For many years, the church (meaning "the people") did not even have a Bible, but depended upon the bishop or priest to read it, telling them what it said. Thank God for men like John Wycliffe, Martin Luther, and others who thought it important to translate the Bible into the common every day language for people to read. These men sacrificed their lives and reputations for us. Allow God's word to change, shape, and defend your life. Prayer and the Bible combined form the most imposing duo of weapons on the planet. If we will correctly and consistently pray and read the Bible, the opponent does not have a single line of defense against us, but must flee.

Daily Challenge: Memorize a favorite verse from the Playbook so you can be prepared as Jesus was when temptation comes.

PUT IT ON!

"Rather, clothe yourselves with the Lord Jesus Christ, and do not think about how to gratify the desires of the sinful nature."
ROMANS 13:14

It hangs in the locker of every pro athlete when they come to the stadium. When you see a player out of his or her uniform they just look different. We are so accustomed to watching them compete in the uniform. It is a fact that when the uniform is put on, the athlete shifts into another mental mode ready for action. There is just something about wearing those colors and name that alters the sense of competitiveness and drive to excel.

Paul, in a figurative sense, commands us to do the same as Christians-we are to "clothe ourselves with Christ" just as an athlete would put on the uniform. The implication is when we put on the very nature of Christ; it will enable us to overcome the sinful nature still clinging to us. This is an intentional action on our part, for clothes do not go on our bodies by accident. Some Christians choose to "cover up" or "leave off" parts of the uniform so as not to expose themselves as followers when faced with compromising decisions. What happens if an athlete is not wearing the full uni-form? He or she is not allowed into the game, therefore causing the whole team to suffer. Spiritually, new or potential teammates can witness us making compromising decisions, giving them reason to compromise. Put on Christ today and win the battle over the sinful nature in your life.

Daily Challenge: Who is watching your actions today to see if you are real or fake?

WEAR THE UNIFORM

"'Friend,' he asked, 'how did you get in here without wedding clothes?' The man was speechless."
MATTHEW 22:12

In every pro sport, there is that one team whose uniform stands out from all the others. Ask any pro baseball player and fan and they will tell you it is those Yankee pinstripes in baseball. Players that get traded to the Yankees just can't wait to put them on. Players that leave the Yankees don't perform at the level they once did. More often than not, those pinstripes make an average player great. There is just something about the players that have gone before winning championships to make a legend out of those hallowed stripes.

As putting on Yankee pinstripes often changes a baseball player, so Christ's righteousness always changes a person. In this parable, Jesus made it clear how to be on His team. It is an open invitation to all. As verse eleven describes, it is only by putting on the righteousness of Christ. There is no other way. Others may try to show up on their own terms without the uniform, described here as a wedding garment (v12). Here, the Playbook clearly shows in Jesus' words it's not what we do that gets us entrance to the banquet (Heaven), but what we have on in the form of His righteousness. The uniforms are free, yet sadly they are refused, resulting in separation from God (v13-14). Proudly wear the uniform of Christ's righteousness so all may see for whom you play. It just may transform the way you compete in the game of life.

Daily Challenge: How can wearing the righteousness of Christ alter some of your life's choices today?

INTRODUCTION

OPPONENT

In football, coaches spend hours studying film on them. Who is it?…the OPPONENT. Looking at formations, tendencies, and plays, while taking into account their own team's strengths and weaknesses, coaches develop a game plan. The challenge is two-fold: the opponent also has a game plan, and imperfect players must execute a flawless plan.

This section will focus on our opponent(s) in life. One we all know, yet many ignore. He is the evil one, Satan, and he exists to either keep us off God's team or to keep us from being effective on God's team. The other we all know too well. It is the sin nature with which we were born. It never leaves us and constantly wants us to do things out of line with our Head Coach's game plan.

KNOW THE OPPONENT

"Be self-controlled and alert. Your enemy the devil prowls around
like a roaring lion looking for someone to devour. Resist him,
standing firm in the faith, because you know that your brothers
throughout the world are undergoing the same kind of sufferings."
I PETER 5:8-9

The 2004 USA men's basketball team was expected to dominate the
games. Made up of professional players, many believed anything
but a gold medal would be a failure. The perception was that by just
showing up, USA would win on talent alone. Behind superior play
and serious underestimation, other countries with their own pro-
fessionals defeated the U.S. knocking them to a bronze medal.

Just as the USA basketball team overlooked the opponents in
the Olympic games, we have a tendency to do the same in life. How
do I know this? In I Peter chapter 5, we are reminded to be "self-
controlled" and "alert" when the subject of the enemy is mentioned. The day we forget our reason for living is the day the roaring lion (Satan) will come to devour us. Those times when we begin
to feel comfortable in our Christian life, and have the feeling of
having it figured out, is when we are most vulnerable. All the opponent is looking for is one small crack to squeeze his way into our
life. Notice he just doesn't want to nibble at us, but his goal is to
devour. The very nature of the word means, "to do away with completely and destructively." Knowing our opponent should allow us
to never underestimate his abilities.

Daily Challenge: Do you think these verses are a good description
of how the opponent has attacked your life?

OPPONENT'S GAME PLAN

"For our struggle is not against flesh and blood, but against the rulers, against the authorities, against the powers of this dark world and against the spiritual forces of evil in the heavenly realms."
EPHESIANS 6:12

The best game plans are those which are simple, basic, and to the point. There are many ways to say the same thing. The key is for the team to buy in and follow through with what the coach draws up. The first part of any plan, however, is being able to define who you are up against. What the opponent does best and how they try to come at you are key things that must be defined.

Our opponent in life has a very simple game plan, which explains why he is so effective in our world. If you are not on God's team, the opponent's mission is to keep it that way. Whatever he has to do, he will do. If you are on God's team, his mission is to keep you on the sidelines. The sidelines of life is where depression, mediocrity, distractions, fear, etc. all hang out. Whatever will keep us from realizing our true identity and gifts so we will not be a difference maker on the field is his strategy. Paul, in Ephesians, describes our opponent to us. Knowing what our opponent is like will enable us to develop an offensive and defensive strategy. Realizing who is against you is the first step in winning.

Daily Challenge: In what areas of your life do you think Satan may try to get you on the sidelines? Because of a circumstance, does he have you there already?

OPPOSITION IN ACTION

"Some people are like seed along the path, where the word is sown.
As soon as they hear it, Satan comes and takes away the
word that was sown in them."
MARK 4:15

In baseball, stealing a base on offense has taken a back seat to hitting a home run. Base stealing was an art perfected by guys like Rickey Henderson, Vince Coleman, Lou Brock, Ozzie Smith, and Tim Raines. There are still some good ones today, but the big money go to the guys who can hit the home run more often.

Spiritually speaking, there is a hall of famer at work today when it comes to stealing. Here in Mark chapter four, Jesus is telling a story about our job as Christians to spread the good news. He is using the illustration of sowing seeds. One of the four possibilities he gives to seed sowing is that our opponent steals it away before it has a chance to take root. Some of the opponent's techniques are: distractions, getting the intended target caught up in worldly things, a bitter past, and guilt. Whatever he can do to cause someone to ignore Jesus he will do it and he is good at it. Be aware of this action by the opponent. Sometimes just doing our job as Christians and throwing the seed of the gospel out there one time is not enough. Statistics have shown that often people come to know Christ only after hearing the gospel presented to them multiple times. Don't let the opposition discourage your seed sowing by his action of theft. Keep throwing it out there!

Daily Challenge: Do you remember how many times it took you hearing the gospel before you decided to follow Christ?

LANGUAGE OF THE OPPONENT

"You belong to your father, the devil, and you want to carry out your father's desire. He was a murderer from the beginning, not holding to the truth, for there is no truth in him. When he lies, he speaks his native language, for he is a liar and the father of lies."
JOHN 8:44

In a short amount of time, the make up of professional sports in America has changed. No longer are teams made up of players just from the U.S. all speaking the same language. Other countries are also producing world-class athletes as evidenced by players like Yao Ming, Ichiro, Manu Ginobli, and Hideo Nomo. As a result, an issue arises: how do teammates communicate?

On the subject of language, our opponent in life has one in which language he is very fluent. In fact, it takes no effort at all for him to use it because it is his native, primary language. What is it? It is the language of lies. One of his many nicknames is the "father of lies." He will say anything to try and convince us of our worthlessness to God. One of the more common ways is the practice of dumping guilt on us about our past mistakes we have made. He feeds us the lie that our sin is too great for God to forgive and to ever use us again. Nothing could be farther from the truth. We know what the Bible says in I John 1:9 about confessing our sin: we will not only be forgiven but also purified from our unrighteous ways. Don't listen to the language of the opponent, but turn your ears to the truth that comes from God, our Head Coach.

Daily Challenge: What are some other lies our opponent has tried to tell you?

THE TEMPTER

"Then Jesus was led by the Spirit into the desert to be tempted by
the devil. After basting forty days and forty nights, he was hungry.
The tempter came to him and said…"
MATTHEW 4:1-3A

Though they have been around for a while, just in the last five years
performance enhancing drugs have gotten more publicity. They
have evolved from a simple needle or pill to, in some cases, a high
tech cream and masking agents. It is all in the nature of "win at all
costs" and the ultimate desire of many to perform better, which
ultimately gains them more money. The temptation is also there to
produce, and if you do not, then someone younger will take your
job.

Another character trait of our opponent in life is he is the
"tempter." Whatever area in which you may compromise, he will
attack. We see him at work here in the gospel of Matthew as he is
working against our personal Head Coach. Satan gives Jesus three
different types of temptations where He could have compromised.
All three times, Jesus gives us the model to follow when we ourselves are tempted. He answered back with truth from the Playbook. In order to do that, we first must know the Playbook. If it was
important for Jesus to know it in overcoming the tempter, would-
n't you think it would be important for us? Realize the tempting
nature of our opponent and prepare accordingly.

Daily Challenge: Are you prepared with enough truth from scripture to stand against the "tempter" today?

OLD VS. NEW

"For in my inner being I delight in God's law; but I see another law at work in the members of my body, waging war against the law of my mind and making me a prisoner of the law of sin at work within my members."

ROMANS 7: 22-23

Learning a new system takes time. In football, this is magnified even more. New terminology, schemes, and plays require hours of practice and study in order to excel. What is left from the old system is still there, it doesn't leave. In the heat of competition, when an audible is called, the player must be able to adjust and run the play correctly. If, out of habit, he makes an adjustment back to the old system, usually there is a negative outcome.

We, as Christians, have an "old system" we battle with daily. The apostle Paul is very descriptive in talking about his struggle here in Romans. This "old system" is our sinful nature with which we are born and have our entire earthly life. As Paul described, when we become Christians, we have a "new system" or a new nature. This new nature is to please Christ. These two natures are constantly at war (v23). The good news is that this old nature can be defeated when daily conflict arises (v25). Victory comes not by attending church, doing good things, or being a religious person, but ONLY by allowing the Holy Spirit to guide us into living as the Head Coach would have us live.

Daily Challenge: Can you relate to the language Paul uses in Romans 7?

INTERNAL OPPOSITION

"Do not be anxious about anything, but in everything, by prayer and petition, with thanksgiving, present your requests to God. And the peace of God, which transcends all understanding, will guard your hearts and your minds in Christ Jesus."
PHILIPPIANS 4:6-7

One of the more interesting times when an athlete wins a championship is the post game interview. Two of the common things you hear are: "It just hasn't all sunk in yet," and "We are going to do it next year." Interesting, because you would think after all the hard work, sacrifice, and discipline it took to achieve such an accomplishment you would hear something different. Something like, "I am so satisfied!" or "This championship completes my life." We don't hear this because no number of championships or accomplishments can give the athlete ultimate peace.

We have already studied our external opponent in life: Satan. As mentioned in the introduction we also wage battle against an internal opponent: ourselves. In the illustration above, allowing a sport or a thing of the world to give us our significance and identity will leave us empty. Paul instructs as we follow the game plan laid out for us, our lives will be filled with unexplainable peace from the Head Coach himself. This peace will be a guard to our heart and mind keeping the doubts of our flesh in check. One of the great foreshadowing of Jesus refers to Him as the "Prince of Peace" (Isaiah 9:6). Are you allowing the "Prince of Peace" to do His work inside your life?

Daily Challenge: Have you ever had that empty feeling after a great accomplishment?

Not Your Own

"Do you not know that your body is a temple of the Holy Spirit,
who is in you, whom you have received from God? You are not
your own; you were bought at a price.
Therefore honor God with your body."
I Corinthians 6:19-20

Professional athletes' contracts are known to contain strict rules of what a player cannot do. The organization is making a big investment in them and their talents and wants them healthy. Things such as skiing, motorcycle riding, horseback riding, and hunting are usually off limits. Once that contract is signed, the athlete no longer has free reign to do whatever he or she wants, whenever he or she wants.

This is the same idea Paul is talking about when addressing the people of Corinth. The subject in this part of scripture is dealing with sexual immorality, but the principle applies in all areas of our lives today. He is reminding them when they decided to follow Christ, they gave up the right to do whatever they wanted, whenever they felt like it. Specifically, this applied to their body, or as Paul calls it the "temple of the Holy Spirit." We belong to Team Jesus and we are to live like it. Our old self never leaves and will creep up wanting us to revert back to the ways we used to live before knowing Christ. If we allow this to happen, it will. Allowing the Holy Spirit to be at work inside of us is our only hope of keeping it in check. Just as a pro athlete is subject to his or her organization, we too, are to honor our commitment to follow Christ.

Daily Challenge: Consider the "price" God paid for your soul. Does it compel you to live any differently today?

77

FREEDOM TO SERVE, NOT SIN

"You, my brothers, were called to be free. But do not use your freedom to indulge the sinful nature; rather, serve one another in love."
GALATIANS 5:13

Many fans believe that professional athletes receive preferential treatment. Some might even say high school athletes do. The fact is the athletic world is held in high esteem today on almost all levels. Yet even from high school, some athletes are conditioned to think the whole world revolves around them. Just in the last ten years, we have had athletes on trial for all kinds of crimes who get off completely or receive a minimal punishment.

We have a great freedom on God's team. But as Paul writes in Galatians, it is a freedom to serve others. It is not a freedom to go do whatever we want, whenever we want-all the while knowing God will forgive us and all will be okay. Notice here, as we have studied, the sinful nature is still present. It is very easy to get caught up in sin and justify it by saying to yourself, "I will just confess it at the end of the day." At the same time, we are called to be free-not to live by a set of religious rules and codes. If that were the case, then there would be no reason for Jesus to have come. There was already a system in place that the Jewish people had tried to observe for years before Jesus came. They could not do it. He came to save us and free us from the law. Live in freedom; enjoy this time God has given you on earth by loving on and serving others.

Daily Challenge: Are you guilty sometimes of putting your Christian walk into a set of religious rules and guidelines to follow?

NO ENTRY

"In the same way, count yourselves dead to sin but alive to God in Christ Jesus. Therefore do not let sin reign in your mortal body so that you obey its evil desires."
ROMANS 6:11-12

In the fall of 2004, Ken Caminiti became the latest of star athletes to be conquered by addiction. He was a talented, hard-nose, third baseman who many said was one of the "nicest guys you would ever know." How does a former league Most Valuable Player who seemingly had it all, lose it all? Addiction is no respecter of persons. It does not care how many accomplishments you have, who your family is or what is in your bank account. Its only goal is to ruin your life by playing off our natural human desires and luring us in.

This is why the writer of Romans pleads with us: "do not let sin reign in your mortal bodies." (V12) He knows once we allow it to have an entrance, it is our natural tendency to want more and go farther. It could start by simply looking at a Sports Illustrated swimsuit issue "with the guys" or in secret and from there, grow into a craving you do not want and cannot control. What's the answer? Be busy doing God's work. "Offer your body to Him as instruments of righteousness." (V13) When we are busy doing God's work, we are more in tune with Him. Consistently choosing to follow Christ will strengthen that new nature and make it easier each time to resist the old. Don't allow sin to have an inch in your life today, it will not be satisfied with a small amount.

Daily Challenge: Is there anything in your life that needs to be taken out before it turns into something more?

COACHING STAFF

One of the key elements of a successful team is a coaching staff that communicates and works well together. The head coach gets the attention, but without those assistants multi-tasking in different roles, the team suffers. Consistent and successful teams have coaching staffs that stay together and are genuine friends off the competition grounds.

This section is a study on our Heavenly coaching staff. They are so close and in tune with each other that they are referred to as the "Trinity." They do not function apart from each other. There is God the Father, who is the Creator of this world and architect of our salvation. He is seated in Heaven yet fully aware of all things on earth. Then there is Jesus, God's Son who lived a sinless life here on earth being both man and God. He is the Savior, the One who carried out the Father's plan here on earth for our salvation. He is also in Heaven awaiting the Father's signal to come to earth and take us into eternity. The last or most overlooked part of the Trinity is the Holy Spirit. He is the One we depend upon daily for help. The Holy Spirit is the Helper Jesus left for us on earth as He ascended into Heaven. His roles include: convicting our hearts, revealing God's plan, and enabling us to live the life of a Christian on a daily basis by existing inside our very lives. Let's take a look and study our coaches in life.

STAYING TOGETHER

"There are different kinds of gifts, but the same Spirit. There are different kinds of service, but the same Lord. There are different kinds of working, but the same God works all of them in all men."
I Corinthians 12:4-6

In the 2005-2006 NFL season, the New England Patriots had an obstacle no other team in the NFL was facing. Winning three of the last four Super Bowls, they were faced with the promotion of their defensive and offensive coordinators to head coaching jobs at other places. What had been a successful trio of Belichick, Weis, and Crennel, was now minus the latter two. This is something that happens all the time in sports as successful teams lose coaches to other teams wanting to copy their success.

As introduced earlier, we have a Heavenly coaching staff called the "Trinity." They have been working together for thousands of seasons experiencing great success. Everything They do is in complete harmony. No matter the level of success, splitting up is never an option. Rather, it is to function together-instructing, encouraging, and disciplining us to get out there in the game of life and make a difference. Notice the very nature of a "Trinity" represents the figure of a triangle. Not one of its members is self sufficient on their own. They must function together to be complete. Be glad there is no power struggle in our Heavenly coaching ranks. Follow their example today by just simply being faithful and obedient where They have placed you. If God so chooses, He will promote you.

Daily Challenge: Why are we so eager to get "promoted" in life to greater positions of status?

COACH SPEAK

"For since the creation of the world God's invisible qualities-his
eternal power and divine nature-have been clearly seen,
being understood from what has been made,
so that men are without excuse."
ROMANS 1:20

Coaches are loaded with slogans and statements to motivate play-ers. On top of that, is terminology even the average sports fan would not be able to understand. All of it comprises a term called "coach speak." It is language used to describe movements and plays for the team. It could be a buzzword for a particular game on which the coach wants the team to focus. Most, if not all, is full of wisdom like, "People never care how much you know until they know how much you care." It is the simple things coaches do which athletes may not realize in the moment, but looking back they can see evi-dence of, which helped shape the athlete's life.

Often times in our society, we fail to see (or choose to ignore) our Heavenly Head Coach at work in our lives. Is He too busy to be involved and interested in our little world? As a friend of mine once said, "Not even close!" All we must do is look around and see with our own eyes His great work. This is what the apostle Paul points out in Romans. His creation, a changed life, and His provision are just three areas that prove His existence and involvement in our lives. It is His way of "coach speak" to us. The greatest Word He ever spoke to us was the sending of His son to die for us.

Daily Challenge: What are other ways you can hear & see the Coach speaking to you?

FULFILLING THE ROLES

"But when the kindness and love of God our Savior appeared, he saved us, not because of righteous things we had done, but because of his mercy. He saved us through the washing of rebirth and renewal by the Holy Spirit, whom he poured out on us generously through Jesus Christ our Savior, so that, having been justified by his grace, we might become heirs having the hope of eternal life."
TITUS 3:4-7

A team in sports is made up of all kinds of players with different abilities. This is also true when talking about the coaching staff for a team. In professional baseball, the manager may call the shots, but he will not be successful if the pitching coach is hanging out with the hitters all day. He needs to be working with his pitchers getting them ready for game situations. The same is true for the hitting, bullpen, bench, third base, and first base coaches. Each is put into a position for a specific ability and for the team to function.

This is similar to how our Heavenly coaching staff functions. Each has a role and no coaching staff in the history of time performs better. Here in Titus, Paul puts the Trinity together giving us a glimpse of them all at work. God the Father displays mercy, kindness, and love. Jesus, being the human form of God, makes the greatest save by laying down His life and rising again. The Holy Spirit, gives the evidence of our salvation by renewing us daily and being the down-payment of future promises. The very nature of all three is to be all-knowing, ever-present, and all-powerful. Are there any better qualities to describe someone than these?

Daily Challenge: What is keeping you from throwing down your fear and living in faith with a coaching staff like this?

PASSING THE TORCH

"As Jesus went on from there, he saw a man named Matthew sitting
at the tax collector's booth. 'Follow me,' he told him,
and Matthew got up and followed him."
MATTHEW 9:9

Bill Walsh was one of the greatest coaches in the NFL. Having multiple championships and being in the NFL Hall of Fame will earn you the "great" description. Even though he does not coach any more today, he still gets a lot of recognition. It comes now in the form of coaches to whom he passed down his knowledge like: John Gruden, George Seifert, Mike Holmgren, and Steve Mariucci to name a few. The true mark of a "great" coach is when people want to copy what they do.

When it comes to training someone to take your place some day, Jesus Christ is the best example we have. Besides coming to die on the cross for our sins and overcoming death, pouring His life into 12 men to take this message to the world was His top priority. They were ordinary men, and Jesus taught them and modeled for them how to love others. He displayed to them how to listen, to work hard, and to even endure suffering for doing good. Those 12 men went on to change the world so that the life Jesus lived still motivates and instructs us today. Isn't it great to know we have a Head Coach who trusts us enough to carry the gospel to others? He longs to pass the torch on to you so you can carry it to someone else.

Daily Challenge: Do you have someone pouring spiritual truth into your life? Is there someone you could be pouring yourself into?

Working Together

"May the grace of the Lord Jesus Christ, and the love of God, and
the fellowship of the Holy Spirit be with you all."
II Corinthians 13:14

During my growing up years, the best coaches I played for were not
the ones who had the most knowledge. Why? I can't even remember
their names. The best coaches were the ones who were concerned
about me as a person more than my athletic performance
on game night. They showed genuine concern for my family,
future, and well-being. They were also men of character, though
not perfect, they modeled what it was to be responsible and work
hard. They pushed me to get better, and encourage me all the way.

God, Jesus, and the Holy Spirit function in a very similar way.
They each have qualities that are different, yet work in perfect harmony.
At the heart of their entire game plan you will find us. God
loved us enough to create us and send His only Son to die for our
sin. Jesus displayed the ultimate form of grace by forgiving us, even
though He knew many would still reject Him. The Holy Spirit is
present and at work in the lives of Christians giving us fellowship
with God. The purpose of the Trinity is to work together to change
you and me so we will go out and share who They are with others.
In the process of becoming more like Jesus (sanctification), we are
made into better sons, daughters, husbands, wives, fathers, and
mothers. Allow your spiritual Coaches to work together in your life
today.

Daily Challenge: Do you believe in the "game plan" that God has
for your life?

LIVING IN OUR SHOES

"This is how we know what love is: Jesus Christ laid down his life
for us. And we ought to lay down our lives for our brothers."
I JOHN 3:16

Coaches come in all shapes and sizes. Some have been at it for years, while others are just starting out. Though they love to copy each other's ideas, they also are unique in allowing their personality to come out as they teach and instruct. What is one thing most, if not all coaches have in common? They have played and competed in the sport they are coaching. They know what it feels like to win and lose. They have lived in the very shoes of the athletes they now coach.

This is exactly what Jesus did for us. He is the only member of the Trinity to take human form and go through life on earth (Philippians 2:7). He was born of a woman and he grew up with younger brothers and sisters. He was tempted just like we are, yet was sinless. While here on earth, He gave two simple command-ments: to love God and to love others. He didn't just command us to do it, but gave us the best demonstration of love that has ever been given. He laid down His life willingly on the cross. Jesus, who had it all, gave it all up for us. What a comfort to know we have a spiritual coach that was faced with the same things with which we are challenged today. He endured every one of them by living here on earth. Go to Jesus today and see if He does not have an answer for how you are to live.

Daily Challenge: When tempted today, remember how Jesus responded and do the same. (Matthew 4:1-11)

EVIDENCE OF THE SPIRIT

"But the fruit of the Spirit is love, joy, peace, patience, kindness, goodness, faithfulness, gentleness and self-control. Against such things there is no law."
GALATIANS 5:22-23

Throughout the course of a season, it is interesting to watch teams develop. Players mature and become confident through success, or they begin to doubt their abilities because of failures. One dynamic seems to always ring true: teams end up taking on their coach's personality and spirit. If the coach is "laid-back" in nature, then the team seems to pick up on that and adopt the same mindset. This could be a positive, if the team is made up of young, talented yet inexperienced players who may need patience as they mature and learn. Whatever type of person the coach is it will filter into the spirit of the team giving them an identity.

This passing on of the coach's identity also rings true in our spiritual lives. Once we join God's team, we begin the life-long process of taking on His spirit. In fact, it is the role of the Holy Spirit to infiltrate our lives and conform us to His image. In Galatians, Paul gives us specific qualities of God's character that are evidences of His presence in our lives. These evidences are listed as love, joy, peace, patience, kindness, goodness, faithfulness, gentleness and self-control. These qualities only come from God; there is nothing in or of ourselves that could cause these to exist. Just as athletic teams compete like their coaches, so we must play life as our Coach did. Allow His Spirit to take up residence in your.

Daily Challenge: Do you display these "evidences" on a consistent basis?

88

INTRODUCTION

DISABLED LIST

As an athlete, it is very frustrating when you can't play because of injury or circumstance. You want to help the team and contribute, but you are not able to go. The time spent in rehabilitation and missed playing time allows for more "thinking time" to take place. Injuries happen to the best of players, even when they are in the best possible condition. This is true of the examples we have in the Bible. For example, Moses, Joseph, Elijah, David, and Paul all went through stints on the sidelines where God was preparing and refining them. Jesus spent 30 years in preparation, an unknown to most, before he came on the scene proclaiming Himself as God's Son, performing miracles and ultimately completing His work in less than 4 years. That's 30 years of waiting; most of us would grow impatient after 30 days!

It is a fact of the Christian life that we will go through struggle, hardship, obstacles and waiting if we truly desire to be a difference maker. Jesus taught it to his disciples, and the Bible lays it out for us. You probably have in your past, or are even currently going through, a stint on the "disabled list." The good news is, "…when we are weak, then we are strong (2 Corinthians 12:10)."

In this section we will study examples throughout scripture of how God works through our weaknesses. We may see those times when we have to take a "time-out" as times for the Master Coach to prepare us for something greater.

ENDURANCE

"Consider it pure joy, my brothers, whenever you face trials of
many kinds, because you know that
the testing of your faith develops perseverance."
JAMES 1:2

Amber Hall knows what it means to endure trials of all kinds. Being
a standout on the Texas softball team, she was poised for a great
junior season in 2005. As the conference season began, Texas was
hosting Kansas when the home dugout bench collapsed injuring
Amber and four others. Over the next few weeks, she played
through pain until learning she had a broken leg. This, combined
with the death of a grandparent, showed things were not going the
way she would have hoped and planned.

In the reference verse today, James, the half brother of Jesus is
calling out to Christians to put their faith into action. In this particular section, he is urging them to consider all trials as joyous
opportunities to develop character, maturity, and perseverance in
their walk with Christ. Joyous trials? It doesn't seem to fit together,
but it can. It did for Amber, as throughout the season she organized
chapel for the softball team. She took every opportunity to live and
share her faith to teammates, coaches and the people with whom
she came in contact. Amber Hall did not abandon her faith in
Christ but she endured.

Daily Challenge: Do you remember a time when you endured
through a trial(s)?

GET FOCUSED

"Yet the news about him spread all the more, so that crowds of people came to hear him and to be healed of their sicknesses. But Jesus often withdrew to lonely places and prayed."
LUKE 5:15-16

It's the middle of the fifth inning and the visitor's scoring line reads: 0 runs, 0 HITS, 0 errors. Everyone in the stadium knows there is a possibility they could be witnessing history--a no-hitter and possibly a perfect game! The funny thing is: in the home dugout, no one makes mention of it. After each inning, the pitcher comes to the dugout to sit by himself, talking to no one. Focus builds with each hitless inning as he continues to withdraw by himself until a hit is given up or the final out is recorded.

Being focused in our spiritual life is much more important than being focused in a baseball game. If anyone knew how important the spiritual focus is, it was Jesus. He didn't just know it, but He modeled it here when He was on earth as one of us. When was the last time you had "crowds" of people following you wherever you went? Jesus' time on earth was short and He had many things to do. He also knew the key to being effective was time alone, getting focused on His Heavenly Father, away from the crowds. This example in Luke was not a one-time occurrence, but the Bible emphasizes it was "often" Jesus went off alone to talk with His Father. Take time at some point today to do the same. If it was important for Jesus, then it most definitely is important for us.

Daily challenge: When was the last time you dropped what you were doing to get alone with God and focus on Him?

Pathway to Character

"Not only so, but we also rejoice in our sufferings, because we know
that suffering produces perseverance; perseverance, character; and
character, hope. And hope does not disappoint us, because God has
poured out his love into our hearts by the Holy Spirit,
whom he has given us."
ROMANS 5:3-5

Often, you will hear a coach describe a player by saying he or she
has a lot of character. In coach-speak, it is translated to mean they
compete hard, clean, will not give up, and act right off the field. It
is easy to teach a player how to develop strength, speed, and needed fundamentals. The question is, how do you develop character?

The apostle Paul has the answer here in Romans…suffering.
Ask any player and they will tell you they learn more about themselves, teammates, and coach while suffering. Whether an injury,
slump, or benching; when they are squeezed, true colors come out.
The pathway to character begins with suffering. It is safe to say Paul
had more character than we may ever have (II Corinthians 11:23-
28). This is why he was more than qualified to write about it. Do
you desire character? If you want the kind the Lord gives, then prepare yourself to go through some suffering. It is a fact of the
process. Only when we persevere through the suffering, will the
character come. Throughout we must focus on our one and only
hope…Jesus!

Daily Challenge: Do you desire Godly character enough to go
through some suffering? Are you going through some character-
building right now?

PERSEVERANCE

"Blessed is the man who perseveres under trial, because when he
has stood the test, he will receive the crown of life that God has
promised to those who love him."
JAMES 1:12

It is the longest of any of the professional sports' seasons. Often
lasting from mid-February until early November. It encompasses
one hundred sixty-two regular season games, and if you are fortu-
nate, your team gets to play in the playoffs. The rest of the teams get
roughly three months out of the year to see their family. Oh yeah,
and then you prepare for next season. The majority of the season is
spent in airplanes, buses, and hotels. Baseball, America's pastime,
has been described as a marathon instead of a sprint. It is those
players and teams who persevere through aches, pains, successes,
and failures that succeed. The prize for those who persevere is great!

At the time of the writing of the book of James, Christians were
going through the aches and pains of professing faith in God-even
to the point of death for saying they were Christians. We may not
experience this level of persecution in America for our faith, but it
does exist in places around the world today. We do experience other
forms of persecution today though. James, the writer, encourages
us to persevere through trials. The promise is a blessing of the
"crown of life" which we will be able to present to our Head Coach
someday. This reward will be far greater than any money, trophy, or
recognition we might be able to gain here on earth. Persevering
through trials does have its' benefits.

Daily Challenge: Who could you encourage with this good news
today about persevering through a trial?

RISING AGAINST THE ODDS

"The Lord will rescue me from every evil attack and will bring me
safely to his heavenly kingdom. To him be glory for ever and ever.
Amen."
II TIMOTHY 4:18

The year was 1935. The American economy and people were struggling. In June of that year, a little known horse lost its 17th consecutive race to start off its career. It did not have a bright future one
could say, which was similar to the prospects of our country at the
time. A year later seeing something he liked in the horse, Charles
Howard bought Seabiscuit for a bottom of the barrel price. Two
shorts years later, in 1938, the horse had risen in the hearts of the
American people, pinning their hopes on a horse rising against the
odds to beat the stout War Admiral-just as people hoped to do with
our great country. Seabiscuit won, setting a crowd of 30,000 into a
frenzy, and giving America hope for the future.

In the book of II Timothy, the apostle Paul is rising against the
odds of his circumstances. He was locked in prison because of his
stand to preach the gospel of Christ no matter the consequences.
He was not going to sit around and be depressed. He was not going
to blame God and get angry. He did what he wrote to the people in
Philippi-"Press on!" (Philippians 3:14) He gave hope to young
Timothy and direction to others to follow Christ no matter the
price. Paul's example helped spark the growth of the Christian
church. While others around him had left, and the circumstances of
his life's work seemed overwhelming, Paul stood firm.

Daily Challenge: Would you tell others about Jesus if it meant jail
time?

SUFFERING

"If you suffer as a Christian, do not be ashamed,
but praise God that you bear that name."
I PETER 4:15

Have you ever been overlooked by a coach or lost your job because of your faith? Have you been rejected by your family because of your faith? Sometimes being a Christian will give you a "soft" label by others. This is especially true in the pro sports world. An NBA coach once said two things have ruined pro basketball and the players that play it: golf and religion. While others may not outwardly say it, their feelings are the same as it relates to Christians who strive to live their faith where they work. Whatever it is you do, if you are a Christian, be prepared to suffer in some way.

Just as we learned yesterday, Peter is talking to people who have been chosen by God to follow Him in obedience (1:1-2). He is educating them about being familiar with suffering for following Christ. Expect it. In fact, he not only wants them to expect it, but when it comes, to rejoice! Rejoice that others recognized the source of your identity. Rejoice in the fact that God's power may be revealed through your life. Rejoice in the opportunity God gives you for your faith to be strengthened. Finally, he says those who suffer for wearing God's name will be blessed. Do you want to be blessed by the Creator of this Universe?

Daily Challenge: When was the last time you suffered for your stand for Christ?

TIME ON THE SIDELINES

"And we know that in all things God works for the good of those
who love him, who have been called according to his purpose."
Romans 8:28

As an All-American college football player at Texas, Phil Dawson
was set up for greatness in the NFL. Draft day came and went with
no calls. Then a free agent opportunity with the Raiders lasted only
4 months and doubt started to creep in. Is this what I should be
doing? Is God closing the door on this chapter of my life? Sudden-
ly, an opportunity with the Patriots came available as a practice
player for the '98 season. Great experience, but any athlete will tell
you they want to play in meaningful games. The Browns came calling in the spring of '99 with a job offer and the rest is history.
Becoming one of the top kickers in the NFL, Phil has endured
injury, and toughest of all, patience to get to where he is today.

If you have ever been "on the sidelines" as an athlete, you know
it is a frustrating time. You want to be out there on the field competing. This is the same thing that happens to us when we go
through trials. We don't understand why. All we can rest in, is the
fact our Head Coach has a plan. He is using the trial to prepare us
for something greater. This is exactly what took place in Phil Dawson's life. He would never have drawn up his career to begin the way
it did. But as Phil trusted, God had a plan for his life and used those
2 years to prepare him for future assignments: the assignments
beyond football as a husband and a father. He is an encouragement
to others experiencing "time of the sidelines."

Daily Challenge: Are you doubting God's plan for your life today?

Time Out!

"Then after three years, I went up to Jerusalem to get acquainted
with Peter and stayed with him fifteen days."
GALATIANS 1:18

Imagine, you have endured years of training to become one of the best at what you do. The "next level" of employers wants to pay you millions for your skills. Yet, you have a commitment to fulfill postponing that next step. This is what Air Force grad and Outland Trophy winner Chad Hennings was faced with as he passed on the immediate reward of the NFL to fulfill his commitment to his country.

The apostle Paul had to endure a very similar time-out. It is a little known verse tucked away in Galatians telling us of Paul dwelling in the shadows of life. He spent three years in the desert of Arabia-very close to where Chad Hennings spent his time. Just imagine, Jesus, the one you have opposed, has just appeared to you; and you decide to serve Him with your life now. You have a brand new vision and desire to proclaim this to everyone. Instead, you must wait and allow God to prepare you for His plan for your life. Three years doesn't seem like much now, but living through those years must have been very painful at times. Are you going through a time-out period? If so, take time today to listen and learn what God may be trying to teach you.

Daily Challenge: Can you think of some time you spent waiting as God was preparing you for something?

UNEXPECTED ADVERSITY

"In this you greatly rejoice, though now for a little while you may
have had to suffer grief in all kinds of trials. These have come so
that your faith-of greater worth than gold, which perishes even
though refined by fire-may be proved genuine and may result in
praise, glory and honor when Jesus Christ is revealed."
I Peter 1:6-7

Allison Lambert grew up in a Christian home and decided to follow Christ at an early age. As she got into high school and college,
God was still there, but volleyball and worldly things began to grab
for her attention. So much so, that these began to take priority in
her life. In her first year of college, things could not have started out
better. She was on scholarship and starting for a division I volleyball team! A few matches in and Allison suffered some unexpected
adversity. A season-ending knee injury forced her to consider the
source of her identity.

This is what Peter is writing about here in I Peter chapter 1. In
addressing Christians, he hammers home the importance of where
we put our faith. It is only revealed by some unexpected adversity
in our life. This adversity comes so we may get back on track in
finding our hope and identity in the Lord, and not in a game, our
appearance, our family name, or amount of money we have. That
was the result with Allison. The injury allowed her to realize she
could be a Christian yet get her priorities out of order. Unexpected
adversity is never fun, but if that time on the disabled list causes us
to get back in line with Christ, then in the end it is worth it.

Daily Challenge: Check the order of your priorities today so you
may avert some unexpected adversity.

REWARDS

Remember all of those award banquets and team parties you went to growing up after the season? More often than not, everyone who finished the season on the team got some kind of award. The concept of receiving awards is Biblical, but the idea that we all will get them is not. As we have studied, entrance into Heaven comes as a free gift with no effort on our part. That is why it is called salvation, for we cannot save ourselves. Beyond salvation, the Playbook clearly teaches there will be rewards for things Christians have done while here on earth. This is what this section is all about. What would a college football season be without the Heisman trophy? As you will see, our Head Coach watches our life to see what we will do with the talents and opportunities He gives us. Not only does He watch, but also He earnestly desires to reward those who use those things for His glory.

CROWN OF RIGHTEOUSNESS

> "I have fought the good fight, I have finished the race,
> I have kept the faith.
> Now there is in store for me the crown of righteousness…"
> II Timothy 4:7-8

Kathy Hahn knows what is means to live out her faith. Choosing to play at the University of Texas gave her the opportunity to play for a top program. What Kathy didn't know was the challenges she would face. Through numerous injuries, she battled through practices and games to compete at a high level, earning conference and all-American honors. With her last year of eligibility cut short, she could have sulked and been upset. Instead, she relied on her faith, poured her time into supporting and ministering to other students and athletes on campus. The God-centered life Kathy lived in college will help her stay the course as she seeks a heavenly crown.

It is a Biblical truth that Christians will some day be recognized for how we live our lives here on earth. What a great feeling Paul must have had, knowing death was close; that he could look back over his life and honestly say he had kept the faith. Just as Kathy was able to do in her college years, Paul did over the span of his life from the time he came to know Christ. As a result, Paul wasn't going to squeeze into the gates of Heaven, but gain what the Bible calls a "crown of righteousness" to be awarded on "that day" by the "righteous Judge." Teammate, "that day" is approaching. Whether by Jesus' return or our days finishing here on earth, our time is less and less.

Daily Challenge: Consider what a joy it would be to lay the crown you earned while on earth down at the King of Kings feet.

PRESS ON

"Blessed is the man who perseveres under trial, because when he
has stood the test, he will receive the crown of life that God has
promised to those who love him."
James 1:12

The Alaskan Iditarod race is one of the more fascinating events of
our time. Led by a musher (name of the person steering the dogs),
teams of Alaskan husky dogs race on snow and ice through extreme
elements over 1,100 miles. It is a race commemorating a similar
life-saving run that took place in 1925 to an epidemic stricken town
of Nome, Alaska. Enduring the elements as a team and finishing the
race is an incredible accomplishment.

The Iditarod is a great illustration of what we encounter in the
race of life. A sudden snowstorm of losing a family member can hit
at any time. An injured dog causes a team to slow down, just as losing a job will affect our decision-making. Here in the book of
James, we are reminded again of the fact that a reward awaits those
who persevere under trial. In times of hardship, we need to keep on
mushing, stay in the race, and keep our faith in Christ, even though
it is rough. Our Lord promises a reward to those who love him. Are
you finding it tough to "press on" today? Remember, we cannot do
it on our own. We must rely on the Holy Spirit and other teammates, especially when times get snowy and treacherous in life.

Daily Challenge: Do you have some "teammates" around you who
encourage you to "press on" in life?

HALL OF FAME

"For we must all appear before the judgment seat of Christ, that
each one may receive what is due him for the things done while in
the body, whether good or bad."
II Corinthians 5:10

Pete Rose was one of the greatest baseball players of all time. Simply being the all-time leader in hits gives him that validation. He also had numerous All-Star appearances, World Series Championships with different teams, and major leagues records. But for what is Pete most remembered? Right now and probably forever, are the accusations and even evidences of Pete betting on baseball games. This is what currently is keeping him from receiving the great honor in the Hall of Fame of major league baseball.

As Christians, one day all our actions will be laid out before God, our Head Coach. In the New Testament city of Corinth, there was a place where the judges of the city would meet the citizens and would judge them for actions they had done. Life or death was not the issue. This is the same type of judgment seat Paul is referring to as it is called the "Bema" seat and still exists today in Corinth. Paul is saying, "we must all appear"-meaning all Christians will stand before God and give an account of what we did while on earth with what He gave us. The question is not entrance into Heaven; rather, it is a stewardship question. We all have unique abilities and resources. Our calling is to spend time doing things of significance with our abilities, which will further God's kingdom.

Daily Challenge: Are there some habits or actions you need to change to make sure you will receive some Heavenly rewards?

NEVER FADING REWARD

"And when the Chief Shepherd appears, you will receive the crown
of glory that will never fade away."
I Peter 5:4

The Olympic games are characterized by outstanding effort and amazing accomplishments. In modern day, the top athletes are awarded a gold, silver, or bronze medal. Did you know what the awards first were? The ancient Greeks and Romans used evergreen leaves and garlands to make a "crown" that was given to the winners of the first Olympic games. This was, however, an award that soon would lose it's color and fade away into a memory as life passed by.

Contrary to these early Olympic awards, the apostle Peter describes our Heavenly reward as one that will never fade away. Those things we do here on earth to expand God's Kingdom will not be forgotten. The reward given by our "Head Coach" will not diminish over time of eternity, but will be remembered. In Acts 7, Stephen had courage to stand in the way of approaching rocks hurled at him as he proclaimed Jesus as Messiah to legalistic religious leaders of his day. In Genesis 12, Abraham had faith to leave what was easy and familiar and trust in God's promise to him with no clue where he was going. Likewise Paul had the discipline needed to pour his life into young Timothy and send him out to do the ministry. These were not perfect men, they made mistakes like you and I every day. But, they, and many others like them, had their eyes fixed on a never-fading reward-to be rewarded at a ceremony growing closer every day!

Daily Challenge: Are you ready for the awards ceremony?

SEEK THE REWARD

"And without faith it is impossible to please God, because anyone who comes to him must believe that he exists and that he rewards those who earnestly seek him."
Hebrews 11:6

College football has become a year-round sport. It is filled with the recruiting season, spring season, summer workouts, and two-a-days which lead right into the regular season. The regular season is capped off with nearly 30 bowl games. Just making a bowl game for some programs is not good enough. Even with a perfect season, a team is not guaranteed a chance to play for the National Championship. Just ask the 2004 Auburn Tigers.

In this season of life, our Head Coach guarantees us a reward. The writer of Hebrews gives us a clear directive on how to obtain it. We are to believe God exists, seek after Him, and live by faith. Are you seeking after eternal rewards? College football programs spend millions of dollars to obtain rewards, sparing no expense. Players and coaches burn the midnight oil and tear down their bodies to win championships. The motivation should be the same for us as members on God's team. We not only will secure a Heavenly reward some day, but also we will have the confidence in knowing we are pleasing the Head Coach. There is no better spot than that in the entire universe. Seeking the reward of a growing relationship with Christ should be our goal. The relationship He allows us to have with Him is reward enough.

Daily Challenge: Are you experiencing the benefits today of a relationship with God?

RUN TO WIN

"Do you not know that in a race all the runners run, but only one
gets the prize? Run in such a way as to get the prize."
I Corinthians 9:24

In the 2000 summer Olympics, there were many outstanding performances. None were bigger than the performances of American sprinter Michael Johnson. Dressed with a fresh pair of gold colored shoes, Michael did not disappoint his fans and country winning multiple gold medals. Michael ran with purpose, vision, and discipline with performances not to be forgotten.

The apostle Paul was a student of the Roman games, an early form of our modern Olympics. Here in Corinthians, he compares living the Christian life to that of a sprinter in the games. Just as the sprinter has purpose, Paul, too, had purpose. Here he was preaching the gospel, starting up churches, discipling young men, and he recognized if he did not live what he was preaching, it was no good. Having the character and discipline to do things as Christ would was his priority. If he did not, he felt he would disqualify himself from the opportunities God had sent him to do. His purpose was two- fold: to see lives changed as a result of his work on earth, and to be rewarded when he hit the finish line of life. Are you running to win similar prizes today? No matter what profession you are in, if you are not running with that purpose, then you are running aimlessly. We are all in the race; it's up to you to get training.

Daily Challenge: What strength will sustain you in the race Paul describes here?

FINISH

"Behold, I am coming soon! My reward is with me, and I will give
to everyone according to what he has done."
Revelation 22:12

In the athletic world, motivation is an often-overlooked ingredient
to winning. Teams have won games with less ability, but who are
motivated to go all out. There is nothing more upsetting than to
know you should have won the game, yet you did not give it your
all. If you had done so, the final score would have been different.
Why is this so upsetting? Because effort is something we all control,
we determine whether we give it all or just show up happy to be
there. The best motivation is always to play each game as if it were
our last. Just as in life, the athlete is not guaranteed another game
tomorrow.

The fact remains, our Head Coach is coming soon and we are
not guaranteed tomorrow. Another fact remains as Revelation
reveals: when He comes, He will bring a reward. Will He be bringing something for you? As Christians, we have motivation to live
life with urgency; yet so many of our teammates live with an apa-
thetic approach to life. Many enjoy a nice sermon on Sunday morn-
ing, eat lunch with the family, and then go back to whatever they
want to do the other six days of the week. Set yourself apart and
commit today to FINISH strong. Many begin the race of life strong
and focused on doing so much for God. However, the ones who finish strong are few and far between.

Daily Challenge: Are you committed to FINISH strong in life?